The
Crusades

The
Crusades

REVISED EDITION

. . .

Richard A. Newhall

Emeritus, Williams College

HOLT, RINEHART AND WINSTON, INC.

**NEW YORK • CHICAGO • SAN FRANCISCO • ATLANTA • DALLAS
MONTREAL • TORONTO • LONDON • SYDNEY**

Preface

The crusades gave new impulse to the writing of history in the Middle Ages. Participants knew they were sharing in great events of more than local significance and felt impelled to write down their experiences. Within a century of the First Crusade one of the outstanding historical works of the medieval period had been completed, William of Tyre's *Historia Hierosolymitana.** In the thirteenth century Villehardouin and Joinville wrote equally distinguished accounts, one of the Fourth Crusade, the other of the crusades of St. Louis.

The point of view from which crusading was treated varied from age to age. For Guibert, the pious medieval author of *Gesta Dei per Francos,* "God invented the crusades as a new way for the laity to atone for their sins and to merit salvation." For polemical Protestants crusading was a device by which scheming popes exploited superstition in order to expand their own power. To Gibbon, the enlightened eighteenth-century rationalist, the crusades appeared as demonstrations of an "obstinate perseverance" which "may indeed excite our pity and admiration," activities in which men of every condition, during six succeeding generations, "staked their public and private fortunes on the desperate adventure of possessing or recovering a tombstone two thousand miles from their country"—all to no avail. For later-day romantics the crusading leaders, such as Godfrey and Tancred, were paragons of heroic chivalry.

Modern scholarship in the past century has stripped from medieval crusaders many of their romantic trappings, finding economic and political motives behind the appearance of religious enthusiasm. Such scholarship also has broadened the field of study by showing that crusading efforts were not solely directed to the recovery and retention of Jerusalem and the Holy Places. The late Professor La Monte defined a crusade as "a war against the enemies of the Church, con-

* William of Tyre, *A History of Deeds Done Beyond the Sea,* 2 vols. ed. and trans. by E. Babcock and A. C. Krey (New York: Columbia University Press Records of Civilization, 1943).

ducted under the auspices of the Church for ecclesiastical purposes, with spiritual privileges assured to participants." Even the social psychologists have attempted to explain the movement in their own peculiar terms. The Muslim world is better known and understood than was formerly the case, and is a matter of more current concern. To look at the medieval crusades from a Muslim point of view can be a helpful intellectual experience and is easier to do for Western readers immune to religious fanaticism. Even in the nineteenth century warlike religious enthusiasm had appeared among Muslims in the Caucasus, the Sudan, and Somaliland.

In certain phases of the crusading movement one may also find early forms of that economic expansionism which eventually grew into what is now referred to as "colonialism." This is not to suggest that the modern question can be more clearly understood by studying its medieval background. Rather, the fact of historical continuity serves to show that when men in the past were faced with certain conditions, they tended to manage affairs to their own advantage within the framework of those conditions. When the conditions changed new ways of pursuing self-interest were needed. But no great effort of the imagination is required to see similarities between some of the crusaders in the eleventh and twelfth centuries and the conquistadores in the sixteenth, or between the Venetians in the Levant and the later merchant adventurers. It can also be urged that modern French statesmen, with popular support, have claimed for France a preponderance of influence in Syria and tried to re-enforce such claims with reference to the crusades.

Crusading was only part of medieval history, and was seldom the most important part, although often one of the most dramatic. An effort to relate it to other contemporary interests and activities, in a brief treatment, is necessary but is almost certain to seem highly inadequate. There were rivalries, even religious ones, in both the Christian and Muslim communities, which complicated and modified the ideological hostility of two irreconcilable religions. Some of these will be noted in their place and the reader is admonished to keep them in mind, even when centering his attention on crusading as such.

Williamstown, Mass.   R. A. N.
January 1963   S. R. P.

Contents

C H A P T E R . . . 1

Christianity
and Islam
before the Crusades

Medieval Religious Warfare

One of the distinctive features of the medieval epoch, distinguishing it sharply from other periods of European history, is the religious warfare of Islam and Christianity. The initiative in the first instance came from Islam. The duty of war against the unbeliever was an early tenet in Muhammad's preaching and early victories and extensive conquests seemed to prove Allah's support. In some respects this contest appears as a phase of the age-long contest between Europe and Asia, between East and West, but the religious rivalry peculiar to the Middle Ages gave, at times, an ardent energy to the struggle which makes it different from

the Greek and Roman wars against the Persians. Often
enough, on both sides, incentives other than religious
ones played their part, and religion frequently became
merely the cloak for worldly ambitions. Religious enthusiasm was only occasionally sufficient to stimulate
efforts on a large scale, and was often curbed by other
pressing interests of a secular sort. But there always
remained for both antagonists some consciousness that
the war was one between believer and infidel in which
God would assist the faithful.

The original fanaticism of Islam in the seventh century had given the Saracens an impetuosity that carried forward their conquests into western Asia, northern Africa, and Spain with astonishing speed and
success. But the early decades of the eighth century
saw their advance checked in the East at Constantinople and in the West by the Carolingian Franks,
at a time when the Muslim state was beginning to
suffer seriously from those disintegrating forces which,
sooner or later, always seem to appear in Oriental military states. Christian Europe was relieved of the menace
of Muslim conquest, but now found itself confronted
by dangerous neighbors who continued to carry on intermittent semireligious war with varying fortunes at
different points of contact.

There were three areas in which the two hostile
religious communities clashed: in Spain, where the
emirs and caliphs of Cordova ruled most of the peninsula and where the Muslims, when hard pressed, might
be reinforced from North Africa; in the western Mediterranean, where the North Africans conquered the
islands from which they dominated the sea and harassed
the coasts of France and Italy—sometimes even establishing temporary posts on shore from which to pillage; and in the Levant, where Saracen pirates plundered the Aegean islands and the Greek coasts from
Cyprus and Crete, and a continuous frontier war was
carried on from Mesopotamia and Syria against the
Byzantine provinces of Asia Minor. For Christendom,

in addition to these Muslim frontiers, there were also pagan neighbors in central Europe. These were peoples not strong enough to be dangerous, but weak enough to invite aggression in the name of religion. Charlemagne's conquest of the Saxons converted that people to Christianity, and his successors in Germany viewed the pagan Slavs to the east as legitimate objects for similar treatment.

Political-Sectarian Rivalry in Islam

The abatement of a large-scale Muslim attack upon Christian Europe was due more to Muslim political weakness than to European strength. Before Muhammad's own generation was dead, the question of leadership in Islam—of succession to the caliphate—had produced civil war, and wars of succession among Muslims tended to become religious. Division into two major sects, the Sunnites and Shiites, stems from this struggle, each sect regarding the other with intense hostility. In addition, tribal rivalries in Arabia, which antedated Muhammad, persisted and were carried throughout the Muslim world by the conquering Arab armies. The Bedouin Arabs and their Berber counterparts in North Africa, to whom the original puritanical simplicities of Islam appealed, viewed the civilized luxuries of urban life with moral aversion and resented the efforts of a central government to restrain their habitual turbulence. They frequently rose in revolt in the name of primitive Islam. Religious enthusiasts, imitating Muhammad's preaching without pretending to be prophets, appeared on occasion and gained enthusiastic followings, more willing to wage holy warfare against rival Muslim sects, which were near at hand, than against Christians. Indeed, generally speaking, the various Muslim groups were more prone to fight each other than to continue the war to spread the One True Faith.

Within a century of Muhammad's death, Islam had

split politically into adherents of two rival dynasties, the Umayyads and the Abbassids. In 730 the latter captured the caliphate and massacred the rival family. But one fugitive Umayyad reached Spain, where he secured the recognition of western Islam. This broke the Muslim empire in half. In the East the Abassid caliph at Bagdad was a Sunnite, but large numbers of his Persian subjects were Shiite. Furthermore, this sectarian difference took on a new political form when a Shiite dynasty, the Fatimids, established itself successfully first in Tunis and later in Egypt, setting up a rival, Shiite caliph at Cairo. Since earliest historical times Egypt and Mesopotamia had struggled with each other for control of Syria, and the fervor of holy war against the Christians was now somewhat mitigated in the fierce contention of rival caliphs, of Cairo against Bagdad. In the West the lines of cleavage among Muslims were between Arab and Berber, the former—the original leaders—disposed to assume positions of lordship and to cultivate a refined and luxurious culture, the latter—the rank and file of western Islam—resentful of Arab arrogance, fanatical, puritanical, and warlike. The Arab rulers of Spain were quite as much concerned with conditions in North Africa, whence new Muslim conquerors could come, as they were with the Christians in the northern mountains. The Spanish Muslims were Sunnites, so the founding of the Fatimid power in Tunis was a distraction, another possible threat to their position not to be disregarded. In all these Muslim states, the existence of local governors ready to exploit any weakness in the caliphate to become semi-independent, and to fight with each other for territory, was a persistent source of weakness.

The Byzantine Empire as a Military Power

Of the Christian powers the strongest and most persistent champion against militant Islam was the Byzantine Empire. Due to its location in the eastern Mediterranean area, it had sustained the first shock of Muslim attack, which had robbed the emperors of vast territories in Syria, Egypt, and North Africa. The most energetic Umayyad caliphs, whose capital was at Damascus, dreamed of storming Constantinople. Three times Muslim forces attacked the Christian capital (668–669, 674–680, 717–718), but the defenders denied them this bastion of Europe's defenses. Small wonder that the Byzantines regarded the Saracens as the empire's most formidable foe, not so much because they were Muslims as because they were aggressive and strong. Religion might contribute to Byzantine tenacity, but self-defense and self-interest were the foundations of imperial policy. In comparison with the rest of Europe in the Carolingian and feudal periods, the Eastern Empire was the only efficient military state. Its military traditions were an inheritance from the victorious armies of republican and imperial Rome, giving the Byzantine soldiers that professional pride so important for morale. The Byzantine army was a highly organized group of permanent units, well disciplined and better armed than any contemporary force. Recruitment was systematic. Some of the best soldiers being drawn from the hardy peasantry of Asia Minor. The soldiers swore allegiance directly to the emperor, and all the officers were appointed by the imperial government. The military art, both as to theory and practice, was a subject of careful study, and certain of the emperors themselves wrote practical handbooks on the art of war, describing the peculiar fighting qualities of their various enemies and prescribing the most effective ways for meeting each. The disastrous defeats suffered at the hands of the Saracens in the seventh century were due, in considerable part, to the overwhelming numbers and the fanatical enthusiasm of the Muslims, and the boldness and vigor of their military leaders, rather than to the weakness of the Byzantine military system. The real weakness of such a highly developed professional army was its cost, and the impossibility of quick replacement.

The victorious Muslim attacks of the seventh century had put the Eastern Empire on the defensive. Its provincial administration was reorganized on a military basis, the old imperial subdivisions of diocese and province being replaced by military districts called "themes." Regiments and divisions were permanently established in each "theme," and their commander, in addition to his military duties, acted as civil governor of the district. After 718, when the caliph's forces withdrew defeated from the walls of Constantinople, there was no further danger of Saracen conquest, but the Muslims continued to make great plundering raids into Byzantine territory. The local Christian commanders were expected to prevent or repulse these attacks. Consequently, the greater part of the Byzantine forces in Asia Minor consisted of heavy cavalry that could be mobilized rapidly against enemy raiders, and was, man for man, superior to the more lightly armed Saracens. For the most part Christian strategy was defensive. No chivalrous sentiment ever prevailed at Byzantine headquarters. Only barbarians enjoyed fighting for its own sake. For imperial generals, war was merely a means to an end. If the objective could be gained without fighting, so much the better. So while not lacking in courage, the Greeks studied how best to succeed through stratagem, ambush, fraud, and maneuver, calculating the weaknesses of their enemies and taking every advantage of them. Pitting skill and efficient organization against the greater numbers of their opponents, and avoiding wars of conquest, they held their own successfully in persistent border war.

Byzantine Reconquests in the Tenth Century

In the tenth century, however, the Byzantine Empire was able to do more than merely defend its frontiers.

The emperor's autocracy reached its zenith so that his control over the empire's resources became more complete than before. This coincided with the rule of a single dynasty, the Macedonian, which held the throne for more than a century and a half (867–1025), thus eliminating for that period some of the intermittent struggle for the throne that so often exhausted the energies of the state in civil war. The first Macedonian emperor could reassert Byzantine rule in southern Italy after the Muslims from Sicily were expelled from Bari. His successors were able to turn their attention toward the recovery from the Saracens of some of the lost provinces in Asia.

Opportunity for this was found in the decline of the Bagdad Caliphate. The sons of Harun al-Rashid (786–809) quarreled among themselves for the succession to their father's throne and the last of them, to assure more completely his control of a turbulent capital, surrounded himself with a large Turkish guard. This force was recruited by purchasing Turkish slaves (mamelukes) or enrolling prisoners of war, and it served as a permanent military force supporting the caliph's power. However successful these foreign guardsmen may have been in overawing Bagdad, they soon discovered that they could control the caliph himself. During the ninth century the head of Islam became the puppet of his own soldiers. The latter cared nothing for the welfare of the empire. The emirs, who governed provinces in the caliph's name, despised and ignored the authority of the Turkish guardsmen, raised mameluke regiments of their own, and seized occasions to advance their own interests, and enjoy practical independence. In appearance, the Caliphate of Bagdad continued to embrace western Asia. In fact, it had disintegrated into a group of military principalities whose rulers warred with each other more than with the Christians. The emirs on the Byzantine frontier had only their own provincial resources for war against the Eastern Empire and this, with their hostility to each other, gave the Byzantines their opportunity. Even without increased resources of their own they could now hope to launch a successful offensive.

For twelve years in the latter half of the tenth century, under the leadership of Nicephorus Phocas (963–969) and John Tzimisces (969–976), a holy war against the infidels was waged victoriously. These two came from the landed aristocracy of Asia Minor, the region most exposed to Saracen attack. Their military training had been gained in command of the themes on the Muslim border. By marriage with a widowed empress of the Macedonian dynasty, they secured the imperial throne without subjecting the state to the dangers of civil war. From 961 until 975—despite renewed difficulties with the Bulgars to the north—in a succession of naval and military campaigns, they regained Crete and Cyprus, crossed the Taurus mountains into Cilicia and Syria, besieged and captured Antioch and Edessa, reduced Aleppo to vassalage, marched triumphantly through Syria receiving the submission of Damascus, invaded Mesopotamia, and even threatened Bagdad. Not since the Emperor Heraclius conquered the Persians just before the rise of Islam had Roman arms been so successful, and Constantinople again celebrated a triumph. The Byzantines had recovered control of the Aegean, and could hope to extend still further their territory in Asia. In southern Syria they encountered the formidable opposition of the Fatimid caliph of Cairo, which prevented the capture of Jerusalem. In the early eleventh century, however, the later Macedonian emperors were able to extend a sort of protectorate over the Holy Places, but when they attempted to regain Sicily as they regained Crete, they failed. These events do not seem to have attracted any great attention from the Christians of western Europe, but they serve, in part, to explain the Byzantine attitude toward the crusaders. Not only were the provinces of western Asia ancient possessions of the Roman Empire, but they had been, to a considerable extent, already recovered and held until shortly before the First Crusade.

Muslim Conquest and Christian Reconquest in Spain

In Spain, Christian resistance to the Muslim conquerors had persisted from the time of the original Arab invasion in the early eighth century even though crowded into the northern mountains. A special feature of Spanish history is the development in the ninth century of three different centers of Christian recovery: the Asturias in the west, the forerunner of the kingdom of Castile-León; Navarre in the center; and in the east, Charlemagne's conquest, the Spanish March and the county of Barcelona, nucleus for the future kingdom of Aragon. In each of these states questions of hereditary succession, of feudal resistance to growing royal power, and of ambitious plans for territorial expansion not necessarily at Muslim expense served to distract from the incipient struggle for Christian reconquest of the whole peninsula. In the intermittent border warfare both Muslims and Christians had small compunction in seeking allies or accepting aid from each other in political struggles with their coreligionists. Under a strong ruler the Moors sometimes attacked and defeated the Christians, but such efforts were more in the nature of punitive expeditions rather than attempts at permanent conquest. When Moorish rulers were weak and the Muslims disunited, one or another of the Christian states could exploit the situation to expand its frontiers, but united action by all of them was difficult to effect. The process of Christian reconquest, consequently, was slow and halting, the urge to fight enthusiastically for the True Faith being only one element in the situation.

One matter significant for the future was the discovery in Spain in the mid-ninth century of bones alleged to be those of the apostle St. James the Greater.

(In 1884 the Congregation of Rites in Rome stated that these were in fact the remains of the saint.) According to early tradition, this apostle had preached Christianity in Spain. A shrine for these relics was established in the extreme northwest of the peninsula at Compostela. In the course of time this church of Santiago de Compostela became a religious center for Spanish Christendom, an object of pilgrimage for western Europe, a stimulant for the Christian war against Islam, a source of revenue for the Spanish church, and eventually a feature of crusading propaganda.

In 929 the Emir Abd-er-Rahman III of Cordova (912–961), a descendant of the original Umayyad refugee, proclaimed himself caliph, thus adding a third claimant to the leadership of Islam. His rule coincided with the period of Byzantine revival in the East. It marks the zenith of Muslim greatness in Spain. During a reign of nearly half a century this ablest of the western caliphs established a successful despotism, such as was necessary to hold together the turbulent and factious elements of Moorish Spain. His work was well continued by his grandson's chief minister Almanzor, who was the actual ruler during the last part of the tenth century. Under his energetic leadership the Muslims dominated the Christian states of the north, León, Castile, and Navarre. These latter were often torn with civil war. They quarreled with each other, and defeated leaders among the Christians seldom refrained from taking refuge or seeking assistance in the Moorish capital at Cordova. In the course of intervening in the affairs of the northern states, Almanzor, at one time or another, captured León, took Barcelona by storm, and even sacked the shrine of Santiago de Compostela, carrying off the bells to be used as lamps in the mosque at Cordova. Many Christian nobles participated in this raid on Compostela. Almanzor seems to have been content to chastise the northern kingdoms without attempting to conquer them. When he died in 1002 the Muslim power collapsed as rapidly as it had grown. The Umayyad caliphs at Cordova, being personal nonentities, became tools in the hands of Almanzor's sons, like their Abassid rivals and the Turkish chieftains at Bagdad. Those sons struggled with each other and with other Spanish emirs for the control of the Moorish state. The belief that a caliph must be of the tribe of Muhammad prevented Almanzor's successors from seizing the throne and assuming the title of caliph. When, in 1031, the Umayyad family died out, the western caliphate was abolished. Each local emir became free to set up for himself, and the Moorish empire in Spain broke up into numerous principalities. This ended Muslim military superiority over the Christians, and gave the latter their chance to recover the peninsula, an opportunity for aggressive action, which, in the course of the eleventh century, they began to exploit.

In this same century feudal society in France developed to a point where conditions conducive to some sort of adventurous expansion developed. It was a warrior society, and fighting was regarded as man's chief and most honorable activity. Local warfare was more or less the ordinary state of affairs, despite attempts by the Church to impose restrictions. More effective were the efforts of such vigorous feudal rulers, as the dukes of Normandy, who took drastic measures to assert their authority and maintain law and order in their domains by curbing the private warfare of their vassals. When successful, these efforts could excite discontent among the vassals and produce victims of ducal justice, either fugitives or exiles, who would be seeking elsewhere a means of military livelihood. Then, too, the institution of inheritance by primogeniture produced a situation in which younger sons had to seek their fortunes wherever opportunity offered. The more adventurous were prepared to go far afield. It is noteworthy that three areas in the early eleventh century attracted members of these groups, namely, Spain, southern Italy, and the Byzantine Empire. William of

Normandy's conquest of England may be regarded as
something similar on a larger scale, although under
more rigid control, than elsewhere.

The reign of Sancho the Great, King of Navarre
(1000–1035), marks the emergence of a Christian kingdom covering the northern third of the Spanish peninsula at a time when the Cordovan state was in
decline. His family connections north of the Pyrenees
gave occasion for drawing fighting men from France
for frontier warfare with his Moorish neighbors. It is
interesting that the earliest name in the record that
survives is that of a Norman. We glimpse here the
discovery by French feudal adventurers that Spain was
a profitable field for their energies. This is also the
period when the Cluniac reform was introduced into
the Christian kingdoms of the peninsula. Beginning
in 1018 were a series of warlike enterprises led by
barons of Burgundy and southern France against the
Spanish Muslims, captained by the local Christian
rulers. Some of these Frenchmen carved out principalities for themselves; others became mercenary
captains serving either Muslims or Christian rulers in
the local wars of the peninsula. The interest of the
abbots of Cluny in Christian Spain stimulated pilgrimages to the shrine of Santiago. Cluniac priories
along the roads to the south provided hospitality for
pilgrims. For the Cluniacs, Spain was an outpost
against the infidel and their influence may well have
given to the exploits of adventurers some of the
character of a holy war. The spirit of chivalrous feudal-
ism fighting Muslims appears in the *Chanson de
Roland* probably composed at this time—an epic poem,
which, when recited in some castle hall, certainly
served to advertise Spain as a field for adventure.
What made this military and religious movement from
France into Spain important was that it coincided with
the first effective union of the Christian states south
of the Pyrenees.

In accordance with common practice King Sancho

divided his kingdom among his sons, but shortly after the middle of the eleventh century the eldest of them, Ferdinand I, King of Castile and León (1035–1065), brought the Christian states again under a single leader by reducing to vassalage his brother of Navarre. This gave Ferdinand the occasion and the resources to avail himself of Muslim weakness. Instead of conducting mere plundering raids, he undertook to reduce the Moorish emirs to the position of tributaries and to annex border territories to his kingdom. His objective was the city of Toledo, the ancient Visigothic capital, second only to Cordova among the Moorish cities. This ambition Ferdinand did not achieve, but he launched that series of campaigns from which the Christian reconquest dates. It must be noted, however, that these expeditions were primarily political, and religious in only a secondary degree. One peculiarity of the struggle in Spain arose from the fact that the urge to expel the Moors by reconquering the peninsula arose from an awareness of a tradition of unity and independence under the Visigothic kings, a sort of vague medieval "patriotism" linked to the struggle against infidels as enemies of Christ. This is the time (1063) when Pope Alexander II sponsored an international expedition, including many Normans, to help against the Muslims on the borders of Aragon. The castle of Barbastro was taken and held for two years, but nothing resulted from this early "crusade." Ten years later another papally sponsored expedition against the Spanish Muslims was organized on which occasion Pope Gregory VII warned that any lands conquered from infidels pertained to the Apostolic See. The king of Castile was not prepared to recognize these pretensions, which suggest that a holy war was expected to extend papal power. The expedition accomplished nothing. For the most part the fighting in Spain was not marked by that implacable hatred supposed to characterize a holy war. Nor were the Muslim emirs any longer imbued with the early vigor and enthusiasm of their religion. Their mutual rivalries were quite as strong as their enmity for Christians, and King Ferdinand and his successors often intervened as the ally of one emir against another. Only when Christian success threatened to become continuous did the Spanish Muslims realize that they needed reinforcements from their North African coreligionists.

On the death of King Ferdinand in 1065, the Christian advance halted while his three sons, among whom he divided his realm, fought with each other to reunite the state. Through the fortunate assassination of one brother and the treacherous seizure of the other, King Alphonso VI (1065–1109) was able by 1072 to resume the war against Islam. His wife, a daughter of Count Robert of Burgundy, was an enthusiastic supporter of Cluniacs, so the bonds between Christian Spain, the Burgundian adventurers, and the religious reformers were more closely drawn. Alphonso, resuming his father's plan to capture Toledo, turned to the Burgundian barons for additional aid. One of his sons-in-law, Henry of Burgundy, became first king of Portugal in the course of this warfare. Pope Gregory VII encouraged the Burgundians to make these expeditions into Spain, and Alphonso accepted papal leadership to the modest extent of substituting the Roman ritual in the Spanish churches for the Mozarabic one of St. Isidore. Castilian policy remained one of intervention in Muslim wars, assisting the emirs against each other. In this, Alphonso was eminently successful. The heroic impression that he made on his contemporaries, both Christian and Muslim, is reflected in the Spanish *chansons de geste,* which picture him as a romantic hero equal to Charlemagne. It is in his wars that Ruy Díaz de Bivar (El Cid Compeador) figures, and the romantic ballads about his career echo the rivalry between the nobles and a strong king, as well as the adventures of frontier warfare with the Moors. In 1082, after an unsuccessful siege of Seville, Alphonso marched in triumph to the very mouth of the Guadalquivir, where he rode proudly into the sea exclaiming, "This is the boundary of Spain and I have touched it!" At the same time he pushed his plans against Toledo by annually devastating the district around the city and by continually harassing the place from neighboring strongholds. In this way the difficulties and uncertainties of a siege were avoided. After four years the exhausted citizens submitted. On May 25, 1085, the Christian king entered Toledo as a conqueror. Muslims were assured toleration of their religion and the continued use of the chief mosque. But two years later one of the queen's Cluniac churchmen became archbishop of the city and demonstrated his religious zeal by occupying the mosque and consecrating it as a church. The Muslims had to be content with assurances that they would not have to endure further encroachments upon their religion.

Christian Recovery of the Western Mediterranean Islands

In central Mediterranean lands, Muslim attack never seriously threatened to become conquest on the mainland, although there were times when North Africans held coastal cities such as Bari and Taranto from which they plundered by land and sea. Incessant Muslim piracy and almost continuous raiding contributed considerably to the confusion prevailing in southern Italy during the ninth and tenth centuries. Local nobles ambitious to extend their power and city-states concerned for their independence and their commerce— both fearful that Byzantine imperial rule would be made effective—were willing at times to seek Saracen allies, and even found it difficult to unite to resist Saracen attack. The islands of the western Mediterranean—Sardinia, Corsica, and the Balearics—had been conquered by the North Africans in the eighth century. At one time or another Muslim raiders had plundered St. Peter's in Rome, burned the Benedictine

monastery on Monte Cassino, and captured the abbot
of Cluny in the St. Bernard pass. The struggle for the
island of Sicily was between Greeks and Saracens,
which the latter brought to a victorious close in 902
by the capture of the last Byzantine city. The Eastern
emperors, with occasional assistance from their Western
rivals, maintained a precarious position in southern
Italy, and continued to cherish hopes of recovering
Sicily. It was the activities of two new powers, however, that gave fresh vigor, in the eleventh century, to
this war against the infidel. These were the rising
city-states of Pisa and Genoa and the Norman adventurers in Apulia and Calabria.

Like other parts of the Italian coast, Genoa and Pisa
suffered attack by corsairs from Sicily and Sardinia.
Genoa was pillaged in 935. Part of Pisa was sacked
in 1004 and another Muslim attack beaten off in 1011.
The nearness of the common enemy also threatened
Rome, for the emir of Sicily in 982 led an expedition
onto the mainland in a jihad against "that dotard
Peter." The pope is said to have preached a holy war
against the Saracens in 1004, promising the island of
Sardinia to any Christian power that would conquer
it. Eleven years later the Pisans and Genoese entered
into an alliance to recover the island for the cross.
Several victorious expeditions were launched, but the
Muslims were tenacious in defense—and the allies quarrelsome—so that conquest was not complete until
1050. This war against piratical raiders soon developed
into a much more extensive struggle, a war of retalia-
tion upon Muslim lands themselves, from which Christians might expect profitable plunder. In 1034 the
Pisans raided a Saracen base on the African coast,
giving their booty to the monastery of Cluny. In 1062
an unsuccessful attack on Palermo, the capital of
Sicily, produced enough plunder to start building
the cathedral at Pisa. But the most important effort
against the African pirates came in 1087 when a large
combined force from Italian cities, at the instigation

of the pope and headed by a papal legate, attacked Mahdia, the Muslim capital of Tunis—an event that has been called aptly "the dress rehearsal of the crusades." This expedition was highly successful. The defeated Muslim ruler agreed to pay a large indemnity, to release all Christian captives, to stop piratical raids, and to admit free of duty all goods imported in Pisan and Genoese ships. These last arrangements indicate clearly that the contest was not solely, or indeed primarily, a religious war. The Italian cities wanted first to protect their own coasts, and then to extend their trade. The Muslims, who willingly used religion as a justification—if they needed one—for their raids on Italy, merely happened to be the natural antagonists that history and geography placed in competition with the Pisans and Genoese.

Meanwhile, conditions in southern Italy were revolutionized by a series of remarkable events of peculiar significance with respect to future crusading. Byzantine rule was an unpopular, foreign, tax-collecting authority, not strong enough to provide effective protection, but actually weak enough to invite aggression from covetous neighbors and insurrection from ambitious Italian subjects. There is early mention of a pope hiring Norman mercenaries, possibly with anti-Byzantine aims. When Bari revolted, the local insurgent leader, while seeking recruits in 1016, is said to have encountered certain Norman pilgrims at a nearby shrine of St. Michael. These pilgrims he employed. Through them it became known in Normandy that southern Italy—even more, perhaps, than northern Spain—was a profitable field for military adventurers. Opportunities offered by frontier conditions, rather than the possibilities of war against Muslims as such, were the significant attractions. Such a situation lured younger sons and impecunious knights seeking their fortunes. The half-century history of the struggle against Byzantine governors, or the quarrels of local lords with each other, is confused and unimportant.

It shows another example of fighting men, hired by
local leaders, discovering how to fight for themselves,
and becoming transformed from servants or allies into
brigands, conquerors, and rulers. By 1060 two Norman
leaders, brothers of the Hauteville family, with bands
of freebooting adventurers behind them, and by a
policy of ruthless, unscrupulous self-seeking, had set
themselves up as rulers—the one, Richard, as prince
of Capua; the other, Robert Guiscard, as duke of
Apulia and Calabria. After the capture of Bari in 1071
these Normans ruled all of southern Italy. In the next
decade they launched expeditions across the Adriatic
into the Byzantine Empire and penetrated as far as
Thessaly. The papacy, at first hostile, recognized them
as rulers, confirmed their conquests, received their
homage, and sought their support against the Holy
Roman emperor and the rebellious Roman citizens.
As allies against the latter in 1084, the Normans sacked
Rome with a destructive ferocity more ruthless than
any the city had experienced. With the Byzantines expelled from Italy, plans for conquering Sicily could
be matured, and in such connection the Normans became part of the Christian war against Islam, although
for the Normans this was scarcely any more holy than
any of their other conquests.

Opportunity for such conquests had long been apparent. In 1038 the Byzantine emperor launched a
great expedition against Sicily. Norman mercenaries
from southern Italy, including two brothers of Robert
Guiscard, served in the imperial army. Muslim power
was twice overthrown in battle and might have been
permanently destroyed had not one of those court intrigues, so common in Byzantine politics, interfered.
The victorious general was recalled, and the Saracens
recovered their lost ground. Twenty-two years later
the Normans undertook the project on their own account. As so often happened, the Muslims were at
odds among themselves. Three emirs divided the island
and quarreled with each other. It was at the invitation

of one of these that the Normans first intervened. The
Sicilian Muslims feared any great assistance from their
North African coreligionists, seeing in it the probabil-
ity of political domination. The rulers of Tunis were
inhibited from taking effective action in Sicily partly
because of the distance in contrast with the Straits of
Gibraltar, but more because of their wars to the east
with the Fatimid caliph at Cairo, whose Shiite beliefs
they refused to entertain, and the threats from the
Almoravides in the west. The Christian population, although not maltreated by the Saracens, were disposed,
until more familiar with actual Norman rule, to welcome a Christian conqueror as a deliverer. A flourishing civilization, comparable to that of Moorish Spain,
made Sicily attractive to the rapacious and warlike
Normans.

Under the leadership of Robert Guiscard's younger
brother Roger, an attack was made on Messina in
1060. This started thirty years of Norman conquest in
the island, a considerable and permanent success at
Muslim expense, but hardly to be characterized as
a crusade. The numbers employed by the Christians
seem to have been small. The war was often inter-
rupted by more pressing events on the Italian mainland. These facts explain why the conquest was so
slow. Not until 1071 could Roger and Robert con-
centrate their resources against Palermo, which they
stormed after a six months' siege. The terms granted the
conquered show how little the Normans were actuated
by religious fanaticism. Muslims could practice their
religion freely and enjoy the use of their own laws
based on the Koran and administered by their own
judges. Perhaps it is significant that Cluniac reformers
and other clergy exercised less influence among the
Normans than in Spain. Invested by his brother with
the county of Sicily, Roger continued the war for
twenty years more. The fall of Syracuse in 1086 ended
all serious resistance, and by 1091 all Sicily was subjugated and Malta occupied. No longer could Muslim

pirates dominate the central Mediterranean. A warlike and ambitious Christian state, in addition to the Genoese and Pisans, could now in its turn threaten North Africa. From now on this becomes an important part of the crusading pattern.

Norman Threat to the Byzantine Empire

It was not only against infidels that the Normans were disposed to wage wars of conquest. While Roger was gaining Sicily Robert Guiscard was capturing the last Byzantine cities in Italy. In order to take Bari and Palermo the Normans were forced to build a fleet, and in so doing they became a naval as well as a military power. Masters of southern Italy and Sicily, they looked for new lands to conquer. To the north were the states of the Church, an easy prey to a sufficiently un-scrupulous leader. Small wonder that even the boldest popes feared their Norman vassals and allies. If Norman aggressive acquisitiveness could be turned in some other direction, against infidels or schismatics, papal terri-tories would be less threatened. When the Macedonian emperor Basil II died in 1025, the princely families and ambitious generals at Constantinople competed for the imperial throne for more than half a century. At one time even a Norman mercenary leader in the Byzantine army seemed to have a chance of occupying the throne. During this period new, dangerous neigh-bors assaulted the empire—the Pechenegs from the north and the Turks from the east. The empire, which had been strong and successful under the great Mace-donian emperors was devastated and thrown into con-fusion until, in 1081, Alexius Comnenus became em-peror. The Normans in Italy had a poor opinion of the Byzantines as fighting men. An invasion of the Balkan peninsula seemed merely an easy continuation of the conquest of southern Italy. There was also the example of Duke William's rapid conquest of England before the eyes of his southern compatriots. At Constantinople, rulers were well aware of the dangerous ambitions of their western neighbors. They sought to restrain these neighbors by suggesting a marriage alliance, by attempting to conclude an alliance with the papacy, by encouraging insurrection against Robert Guiscard in Italy, and by providing refuge for fugitive rebels from his dominions. These moves served to delay Robert, while at the same time they increased his determination to secure peace in his own lands by destroying the supporter of his rebellious subjects. The political difficulties of the Eastern emperors, and the pressure of the Turks on their Asiatic frontiers, gave him his opportunity. It may be that the popes encouraged a Norman advance eastward, both as a diversion and as part of papal policy with regard to the Greek Church.

Schism between the Greek and Latin Churches

In 1054 the pope and the patriarch of Constantinople mutually excommunicated each other. This created a schism between the Eastern and Western churches. Viewed in the historical perspective of modern times, we can see that this was a break never to be effectively mended. But it did not so appear to men of the eleventh century. There had been repeated schisms of similar sort between Rome and Constantinople since the Arian controversy in the fourth century. They had always been healed without seriously impairing the apparent unity of the Church or the leadership of the pope. Ever since Constantine's time there had been fundamental cultural differences between the East and West, which the Teutonic conquest of the West accentuated. The Greeks, with reason, regarded the Latins as barbarians, ignorant of the language of the Gospels and of the greatest Church Fathers. But the preeminence, if not the authority, in the Church of the

bishop of Rome was accepted by emperors and patri-
archs. Since the ninth century, however, there had
formed at Constantinople an anti-Roman party among
the Greek clergy, disposed to oppose papal claims to
primacy, to regard certain Western practices and beliefs
as heretical, to denounce the Latins as "forerunners
of apostasy, servants of Antichrist, who deserve a
thousand deaths, liars, fighters against God," and to
foment schism. This disposition toward schism increased among the Greeks during the tenth and
eleventh centuries because the moral and political
prestige of the papacy became scandalously low, while
the Eastern Church was enjoying a considerable revival due, in part, to the reinvigoration of the Eastern
Empire by the Macedonian dynasty. Knowledge that
the popes in Rome were creatures of upstart senators
or of notorious women, served to increase the con-
tempt cherished at Constantinople by the anti-Roman
clergy and to encourage new efforts to assert ecclesiastical independence. These efforts reached their height
in 1043 when Michael Caerularius became patriarch. He
was a vigorous, ambitious, domineering churchman willing to thrust the issue of Roman jurisdiction to the
fore, overawing an unwilling emperor and defying
papal authority. His action coincided with the presence
in Constantinople of a papal envoy, a cardinal similarly
arrogant and aggressive. The exchange of anathemas
in 1054 resulted. But at that date the papacy was no
longer the poor thing it had been. German emperors
and Cluniac reformers had restored the pope to the
real religious headship of Western Christendom. Leo IX
and his successors had a high ideal regarding the
mission in the Church of the Roman See. They were
prepared to assert all papal claims to primacy and to
enforce their assertions with whatever means might be
at hand. The fact that Cluniac reformers aimed to enforce celibacy upon the clergy tended to increase Greek
opposition. The popes, if necessary, were ready to heal
the schism by force. Gregory VII, one of the most mili-

tant popes, seems to have entertained the idea in 1074 of leading in person a Latin army eastward to reunite the two churches under the Roman pope. Here was a common interest between the papacy and the Normans, a willingness to attack the Byzantine Empire. The hope of restoring ecclesiastical unity while also asserting papal authority probably entered into the crusading policies of the popes.

Relics and Pilgrimages
in the Eleventh Century

It would appear, therefore, that already in the course of the eleventh century, on certain frontiers of Christendom, a successful offensive against the infidel had started, not by any means primarily motivated by religious zeal. We observe also that the popes and the Norman princes for one reason or another unrelated to Islam were turning their attention eastward. It remains to note the elements in the west-European situation that help to explain the popular response to the crusading idea. It should be remembered that the practice of pilgrimage is common to many religions and that Christians as well as pagans indulged in it in the days of the Roman Empire, and that Muhammad enjoined upon his followers the duty of making the pilgrimage to Mecca. To honor God by visiting places hallowed in religious history and making offerings there is a very ancient notion. Such visitation was an act of piety. Prayers offered at such places were presumably more efficacious, more likely to be heard. This idea was often associated with that of miraculous healing, and in an age when disease was regarded as punishment for sin, the therapeutic value of prayer was important. Even in the twentieth century these ideas still have considerable currency. If God showed a disposition to manifest his power more readily in one place than another, the places so distinguished naturally attracted worshippers from afar. Early in the history of the

Church, places associated with the life of Christ or
with the lives of apostles, saints, and martyrs were
reputed to be of special sanctity. The great powers that
those persons exercised while living were believed some-
how miraculously to cling to the places where they
had lived, to their physical remains, or to any object
associated with them. The cult of relics is the natural
consequence of such conceptions and played a large
part in medieval popular religion. The collection of
relics became a matter of increasing importance, particularly in western Europe where none of the events
related in Scripture took place. A victorious Spanish
king willingly accepted from a defeated Muslim emir
the body of St. Isidore as part of an indemnity. Enterprising merchants stole what they alleged to be the
body of St. Mark in Alexandria and brought it with
other merchandise to Venice. These remains are now
behind the high altar in the cathedral of St. Mark.
Wherever necessary, miraculous legend could be used
to explain the presence of saintly relics, as at Compostela for the body of St. James the Greater.

As important as the cult of relics for the increase
in pilgrimages were the medieval developments con-
nected with the performance of penance. Forgiveness
of sins may be even more important for the individual
than bodily health, and more frequently necessary. The
performance of penitential acts imposed by the Church
in connection with such forgiveness was a commonly
recognized part of medieval practice, one that still
persists. The more difficult the act, the greater the
merit. In a time when travel was hard and dangerous,
a long journey, barefooted and begging one's way, was
an act of real penance. Prayers for forgiveness offered
at some saint's favorite shrine would more probably
gain his intercession with God for the sinner, particularly if the latter had endured hardships in reach-
ing the shrine. Miracles of forgiveness—such as the
budding of Tannhäuser's pilgrim staff—fill the pious
legends, along with miracles of healing. In this con-

The Communion of a knight. Sculpture from the western façade of Reims Cathedral, 1245–1257. (*Giraudon*)

nection may be observed the logical practice of sending murderers and other criminals upon pilgrimage. In this way they atoned for their wickedness and secured divine pardon, while the community enjoyed their absence. A turbulent society could make considerable contributions to this category. Even for the relatively righteous, salvation and spiritual benefit could be expected from viewing some wonder-working relic, and if a souvenir of the holy place could be taken home, some of the miraculous sanctity of the shrine might come with it. An eleventh-century development of the penitential use of pilgrimage is the indulgence. This was a remission to the sinner of part of the penance imposed upon him if he visited some special place, a shrine or a specified church. Places with such privileges naturally found themselves popular resorts for pilgrims, and since contrite sinners could be expected to make offerings, other shrines would desire similar privileges. Other encouragement to pilgrimage was the protection and hospitality offered by the Church to those going on pious journey. Hospices, like that in the St. Bernard Pass, were founded along the more popular routes, particularly by the Cluniacs. Merchants and others who had to travel at a time when all roads were dangerous found the garb of a pilgrim useful. Then, too, a returned pilgrim enjoyed the admiration of his neighbors, and was by custom entitled to wear some symbol to advertise his journey, a cross of palm leaves if he came from Jerusalem (hence the name "palmer"), a cockleshell if he had visited the shrine of Santiago in Spain.

The three most popular objectives for pilgrims were Compostela, Rome, and Jerusalem. Of these, the last as a matter of course, was the most important both because of its special sanctity and its distance. The pious interest of the West in the Holy Land goes back to Roman times. Occasionally since then, popes and other Westerners had had appeals for money to restore the churches in Jerusalem. Charlemagne was in touch

with the patriarch of Jerusalem and he obtained permission from the caliph at Bagdad to build a hospice
in the Holy City for the entertainment of pilgrims.
To the Muslim rulers in Palestine, pilgrims were welcome as a source of revenue. Later generations ascribed
to Charlemagne the role of special protector of the
Holy Places, and even made up and told tales of his
own pilgrimage thither. Even King Arthur was credited
with such a journey, something suitable in literature
for any medieval hero.

A really active interest in Palestine on the part of
the Latins seems to begin in the early eleventh century.
Thanks to activities of Italians, Normans, and Byzantines the sea routes were no longer dominated by
Muslim corsairs. When King Stephen of Hungary and
his people were converted to Christianity shortly before 1000, he "made the way [by land] very safe for
all and thus by his benevolence allowed a countless
multitude both of noble and common people to start
for Jerusalem." The Byzantine victories in Syria enabled the Eastern emperor to assume a quasi guardian-
ship over the Christians in the Holy Land, which
was subject to the caliph at Cairo, and this position was confirmed by treaty in 1027. In the West there
appears a reinvigorated piety that may be ascribed to
the spread throughout the Church of the spirit of the
Cluniac reform. Instead of small groups of poor travelers, pilgrims went in considerable bands, armed for
protection and led by counts and bishops. The count
of Anjou made such an expedition as early as 1011
and, in order to expiate his numerous crimes, made
two subsequent ones in the course of his career. According to current report, on one of these occasions
he was permitted to pray at the Holy Sepulcher only
after promising to insult the cross. This act he avoided
by stratagem, and as he knelt in prayer he bit off
with his "iron teeth" a piece of the holy rock, which
he brought home as a relic. The count of Flanders
and two of the dukes of Normandy, predecessors of

William the Conqueror, made similar journeys. The largest pilgrim band of which there is record, numbering seven thousand or more—a real army by medieval standards—set out from Bamberg in 1064. Clearly the popular movement eastward was already of considerable proportions a generation before the First Crusade.

Muslim Revival in the East: the Seljuk Turks

It was at this time that Islam, in both East and West, experienced religious, political, and military reinvigoration that not only made possible new resistance to Christian pressure, but, in addition, accomplished sufficient reconquest of territory to stimulate new and greater efforts by Christian Europe. This revival of strength in the East had no connection in its origins with the struggle against the Byzantines. It resulted, rather, from conditions in Central Asia, and the pressures from that quarter upon the eastern frontiers of the Bagdad Caliphate. This movement out of Central Asia is a feature of the history of western Asia that had already occurred on various occasions and was again to be significant in the future. Sometimes these pressures drove Asiatic pastoral nomads north of the Caspian Sea westward into Europe; such were the Bulgar and Pecheneg attacks upon the Byzantine Empire from the north in this period. When the states of western Asia were weak, these nomads could also move south of the Caspian, but the last to do so were the Parthians in the third century B.C. Domestic politics at Bagdad in the tenth century provided opportunity for the Turks. With them begins a new phase in the history of western Asia comparable to the earlier movement of German barbarians into the Western Roman Empire. Like the Roman emperors and the Germans, the caliphs had been drawing mercenary Turkish soldiers from Central Asia. The Byzantine emperors also employed Turks when they were available.

One result of the caliph's recruiting was the conversion
of the Turks to Islam. For the Turks their new religion
helped in developing a political cohesion superior to
the loose, tribal organization characteristic of pastoral
nomads. Since the Abbassid caliphs at Bagdad were
Sunnites, these new converts accepted the beliefs and
prejudices of that Muslim sect. Unlike the Persians and
Arabs, the Turks had no interest in the speculation
and religious disputing that served to divide the more
cultivated Muslims. The militancy of Islam, the idea
of fighting for the True Faith, appealed to Turkish
warlike habits and interests. By nature they were loyal
and disciplined, accepting the beliefs of their employer
and willingly and ardently fighting his enemies—political or religious, Christian or heretical Muslim—without concern for theological differences. Their natural
aptitude for battle gave new vigor to the holy war in
such areas as there was contact with Christian states,
as well as to more active rivalry with the Shiite caliphs
in Egypt. Individual Turkish chieftains with their warrior bands appeared on the Byzantine frontier in effective numbers as early as 1048. Here the caliph left
them to conquer principalities for themselves at the
expense of the Christian empire.

The political phase of this movement south of the
Caspian began when a Turkish tribe, taking its name
from its leader Seljuk, appeared on the banks of the
Oxus early in the eleventh century. Under Seljuk's
son, Togrul Beg, these Turks received permission to
seek better pasturage across the river. Admitted thus
into western Asia, Togrul Beg seized the occasion to
conquer an empire. In twenty years of warfare (1031–
1051) he made himself master of most of Persia. This
astounding success impressed the caliph at Bagdad. The
latter was controlled by certain Persian princes who,
though Shiites, preferred to show outward respect for
the Sunnite caliph and, through him, direct the orthodox Muslim state. Against these and against the palace
factions that existed at Bagdad, the caliph invited

Togrul Beg and his Turks to intervene. There was no effective opposition to the conqueror. In December 1055 he entered Bagdad and assumed a protectorate over the caliph. Two years later, the latter appointed the Turk sultan and "Right Hand to the Commander of the Faithful," delegating to him the temporal rule over the caliphate, and, in addition, granting him all territories which he could conquer from the Fatimid caliph of Cairo. This brought to an end the anarchy that had paralyzed the Muslim state for more than two centuries. Master of all the territory from the Euphrates to the Oxus, and a conqueror by nature and habit, the Seljuk sultan turned his attention westward toward Armenia for further conquests. He died before anything could be accomplished, but his nephew and successor Alp Arslan ("the Bold Lion," 1063–1072) continued the advance. This brought on a clash with the Byzantines.

Manzikert and its Consequences

Since the middle of the eleventh century the Turks had been troublesome raiders on the Byzantine frontier, formidable in eastern Asia Minor, but not so immediately menacing as the Pechenegs or the Normans in the Balkan area. Because of their numbers and the rapidity of their movements it proved impossible to prevent their incursions, and on occasion they penetrated into the heart of Anatolia. Turkish chieftains desiring to evade the effective authority of the sultan sometimes carved out semi-independent principalities for themselves in Byzantine territory. Alp Arslan's main objective was to effect the union of all Muslim lands by conquering Mesopotamia, Syria, and Egypt. His ability or willingness to prevent local incursions into Byzantine territory was not complete, but he regarded the empire as a possible menace to his rear in his campaigns against the Fatimids in Egypt and desired some sort of truce. At Constantinople the Macedonian dynasty had first degenerated, and then disappeared. The imperial throne was again the object of contention among generals and nobles. Imperial policy was weakened and distracted by the intrigues, jealousy, and treachery of ambitious rivals. Emperor Romanus Diogenes (1068–1072), who confronted the Turkish troubles in Anatolia, was a general of more energy than judgment. He owed his position to his marriage with an imperial widow, but Nicephorus Phocas and John Tzimisces, in like circumstances, had justified themselves in brilliant campaigns against the Muslims. Seljuk attacks in Armenia and Asia Minor seemed to impose upon Romanus the necessity of imitating his predecessors, while the sultan's movements toward Syria offered an opportunity. Three years of preparation culminated in the spring of 1071 in the mobilization of the greater part of Byzantine military power for the recovery of the lost parts of Armenia. Against such a formidable army, Alp Arslan in person led the Turks, although first attempting to negotiate for peace. The two forces came to battle on August 26, 1071, at Manzikert. Through a combination of rashness and treachery the Byzantines sustained an overwhelming defeat. Their forces were cut to pieces. The emperor was taken prisoner.

The battle of Manzikert is one of the decisive battles in the history of the Levant. It opened the way for an ethnological as well as a political revolution in Asia Minor. It dealt the East Roman Empire a blow from which it never fully recovered. It contributed to the situation that inadvertently brought on the crusades. Alp Arslan, on the morrow of victory, could have marched unopposed to the Bosporus. Had he done so he might have forestalled by four centuries his Ottoman successors unless, in the desperation of a crisis like that of 717, the empire had been able to produce another heroic leader like Leo the Isaurian. But the Turkish sultan was chiefly interested in combating the Fatimids in Syria, and he was harassed by troubles in Central Asia. He held the Byzantine emperor captive only a short time, sending him back to Constantinople as a vassal. Here Romanus found a condition of political chaos, due to his military defeat, and a factional struggle in which he lost his life. Alp Arslan's assassination in the East temporarily eased the Turkish pressure on the Byzantines. For the next ten years the Byzantine state was torn by civil war in which contenders for the imperial throne succeeded in destroying such parts of the military system as had survived the disaster of 1071. It is in this period that the Turkish conquest of Asia Minor took place, not in one great expedition, but piecemeal. The new sultan, Malik Shah, the patron of Omar Khayyám the poet and Hassan Sabbah, founder of the Assassins, was more cultured than his two predecessors, a magnificent Oriental prince like the Caliph Harun al-Rashid. He left it to his lieutenants to occupy Anatolia and Syria where resistance, if there was any, was only local. Indeed rival contenders for the Byzantine throne willingly turned to the Turks for help against each other, surrendering provinces to them in return for military aid. The real resistance to the Turkish advance came from the Fatimids of Egypt, who held southern Syria. But in 1076 the Turks captured Jerusalem from the Egyptians. In 1078 Malik Shah's brother possessed himself of Damascus. Soon afterward his cousin occupied Nicaea near the Bosporus, proclaiming himself sultan of Roum (that is, Rome). Seven years later the last remnant of Roman rule in Syria disappeared with the Turkish conquest of Antioch.

More important for the future of Asia Minor than this political conquest was the immigration which followed it. Turkish rule in comparison with Byzantine was not, in itself, unduly harsh. Some of the Christian heretics in Anatolia found it preferable to that of the orthodox emperors. The Greek Church and the Nestorian Christians continued to exist, not without privileges. But the Turkish conquest opened Asia

Minor to the pastoral nomadic tribes from Central
Asia, called Turkomans by the Greeks and distinguished
from the Seljuk warriors. No doubt the Byzantine civil
war was devastating enough, but the influx of barbarous nomads served to intensify the destruction and
check recovery. These shepherds and herdsmen were
unruly, dangerous, and predatory. They made roads
unsafe for merchants, and the trade upon which city
life depends declined. Their interest was in pasturage
and plunder. As they spread over the land, agri-
culture declined; in some areas the soil began to pass
out of cultivation and revert to pasture. Cities became
isolated from each other, finding their economic existence threatened. Eventually people moved from the
cities out into the villages where they could make some
sort of living off the land, and the population began
to diminish. A region that had been a flourishing part
of some European state since the days of Alexander
the Great in the fourth century B.C. became in eco-
nomics and in population a part of Asia. So it still
remains.

Byzantines, Normans, and Venetians

Meanwhile, at Constantinople a decade of political
confusion was brought at last to an end in 1081 by
the successful usurpation of Alexius Comnenus, a man
vigorous enough and clever enough to control the state
and to direct the forces of the empire with some
success against the foes pressing upon its frontiers. It
is important to note, however, that he no longer had
available the old imperial military machine. Even before Manzikert the emperors had employed foreign
mercenaries as part of their military power. The last
of the well-disciplined, highly organized army had been
destroyed in that battle, and its remnants dispersed
during the subsequent civil war. The organization by
themes broke down and disappeared. The Turkish oc-
cupation of Asia Minor cut off a most important

recruiting ground from which the losses of Manzikert might have been made good in some measure. It became necessary for the new emperor to enlist foreign mercenaries for the greater part of his army. For these he turned to northern and western Europe. It is also significant that at the begining of his reign the greatest menace to the empire was not from the Turks, but from the Normans in southern Italy.

By 1080 Robert Guiscard was free to attempt the conquests in the East to which his ambitions and papal encouragement prompted him. In the two following years he and his son Bohemund crossed the Straits of Otranto, defeated Alexius, captured Durazzo, and pushed eastward toward Constantinople. For four years they campaigned in the Balkan peninsula, and their ultimate failure was due not so much to effective Byzantine resistance as to Robert's death in 1085. From the imperial necessities in this war date the trade privileges in the Byzantine Empire enjoyed by the Venetians. The emperor required naval help and feared that the Venetian ships might be turned against him. The Venetian price for their alliance against the Normans in 1082 was control of a quarter in Constantinople with commercial rights vastly superior to those of any other Italian city. The continuance and extension of their privileges in later years was based on this dangerous combination of need and fear. The Greeks and the other Italians were sure to become very jealous of the Venetian monopoly. In altered political circumstances the imperial government was certain to attempt its curtailment or abrogation. The Venetians were equally certain to resist such efforts.

Muslim Revival in the West:
the Almoravides

It was not only in Asia Minor that a reinvigorated Islam again threatened the Christian position. Contemporaneously with the Turkish advance in the East,

a new Muslim menace of considerable proportions appeared in Spain as a result of events in that peninsula
and in North Africa. In 1039 an ascetic Muslim fakir,
Abdallah ibn-Yasin, returning from a pilgrimage to
Mecca, established himself on an island in the Niger
and began to preach the tenets of primitive Islam to
the Saharan nomads. A religious revival among the
tribes of the upper Niger resulted. By setting forth
the simple puritanism of the Koran and the Hadith
(traditions) and by emphasizing the duty of waging holy
war against Sudanese paganism, this new religious
preacher aroused an enthusiasm very similar to that
of a new conversion. At the start he organized a group
of ardent ascetics (al-Murabitun in Arabic). These have
become known in European history as the Almoravides.
Like Muhammad's original followers these fanatics
launched a religious war under emirs appointed by
Abdallah. A large part of the western Sahara was
rapidly subdued. Emphasizing the strict obligations of
early Islam, they destroyed wine shops and musical instruments, insisted on no more than four wives, and
restricted taxation to the alms prescribed by the
Prophet. In 1061 Yusuf ibn-Tashfin was appointed
governor of the newly conquered Maghrib, and in the
following year he founded Marrakech, a new capital
for his empire at what is now the modern city of
Morocco. Making himself supreme ruler of the Almoravides he extended his rule eastward over North
Africa as far as Tunis and assumed the title "Commander of the Faithful." In 1084 he took Ceuta on
the southern coast of the Straits of Gibraltar. This
was just at the time when Alphonso VI was launching
those attacks against Toledo that gave him the city
in 1085.

Hard pressed by the Christians, the Muslim emirs
of Spain saw in Yusuf a possible savior, but one of
whom they were also much afraid. The culture and
luxury of the Spanish rulers was in marked contrast
with the fanaticism and puritanical simplicity of the

African leader and his desert hordes. The Andalusians knew they must submit to either Almoravide or Christian rule, and they reluctantly chose the former. "I would rather be a camel-driver in Africa," said the emir of Seville, "than a swine-herd in Castile." Several times from 1075 on, the Spaniards invited Yusuf to come to the aid of his coreligionists, but he delayed until he felt sure of his control of North Africa. By 1086 he was ready to make the crossing at Algeciras to rescue Islam, to extend his empire, and to impose his strict religious standards on the effete rulers of Muslim Spain. Assembling the Spanish Muslims under the Almoravide banner, Yusuf marched against the Christians. Collecting all available men, including French and Italian knights attracted to his support in his earlier campaigns, Alphonso VI met the new invaders. On October 23, 1086, at the battle of Zallaka near Badajoz, the Christian army was overwhelmed.

It would seem as if the Almoravides could now repeat the original Muslim conquest of the whole peninsula. For the moment the Spanish Muslims were united under a vigorous and inspiring leader, and reinforced by large numbers of religious enthusiasts from Africa. The Christian reconquest was certainly checked. That it was not immediately undone was due to the distraction of Yusuf soon after victory by the needs of his newly won African lands and by his determination to impose his strict religious practices upon the Spanish emirs, whom ultimately he deposed, and to make his rule over Muslim Spain effective before proceeding further against the Christians. For twenty years after the battle of Zallaka, until his death, the Almoravide ruler was busy consolidating his power in Spain and Africa, and in pushing his conquests northward. He never recovered Toledo, but he did move toward the Pyrenees; he subdued two thirds of the peninsula, the region from the mouth of the Ebro to the mouth of the Tagus. In this struggle El Cid Compeador played an active part, providing material for that body of patriotic balladry that became important in the Christian traditions of the reconquest. It seems possible also that Alphonso's appeals for help to the French may have evoked some popular response and brought his son-in-law, Raymond of St. Gilles, south of the Pyrenees in 1087, although nothing significant was accomplished. Toward the end of this period of resistance to the Almoravides, the First Crusade was launched, the assault of a renewed Christendom against a reinvigorated Islam. That it was launched to the east instead of into Spain is probably to be explained, in part, by the greater religious attraction of the Holy Places, by the interests of papal policy, and by a vague Christian assumption that Islam was a unit that could be attacked equally well at any point.

C H A P T E R . . . 2

Early Crusades

Byzantine Emperor and Roman Pope in 1095

The historian Gibbon, with the hindsight upon history of an enlightened eighteenth-century writer, likened the Emperor Alexius to a Hindu peasant who, after praying for water, was overwhelmed by the flood sent by the too-generous gods in response. Modern scholars, attempting to think in terms of the later eleventh century, make the connection between an appeal from Constantinople and the launching of the crusades somewhat more complicated and less definite than this comparison might suggest. In the nature of things, relations between the emperors and the popes after 1054 were concerned with the possibility of healing the schism of that year, which for contemporaries had no necessary appearance of permanence. As early as 1062 discussion of the issues was opened. Again, shortly after Manzikert, an imperial letter to Pope Gregory VII linked the problem of ec-

clesiastical reunion with military help against the Turk.
At this time the pope formulated the idea of a Christian army, possibly under his personal leadership, to
go to the aid of the Byzantine Christians in their
perilous plight, and urged Raymond of St. Gilles and
Godfrey of Lorraine among others to join such an
expedition. Later he concluded that the danger had
passed. Gregory was not one to abate papal claims,
and when no results followed negotiation he gave his
blessing to Robert Guiscard's attack on the schismatic
Greeks. It is not unreasonable to think that for reforming popes like Gregory and his successors church
unity under papal leadership was a matter as pleasing
to God as the recovery of the Holy Sepulcher from
infidel hands after four centuries of Muslim possession.
From this eleventh-century schism until the eve of the
final Turkish conquest of Constantinople in the mid-
fifteenth century, the issue of healing the schism by
Greek submission to the pope was associated closely
with the possibility of Western help against the Muslim
enemy in the East.

When in 1081 Alexius Comnenus brought to an end
a decade of civil war, he was faced with very serious
dangers. The Turkish threat in nearby Asia Minor,
instead of evoking Christian sympathy in the West,
was regarded by the Normans as an opportunity for
invading the empire. By coming to terms with the
neighboring Turks, followed later by a temporary alliance, and by skillful diplomacy in the best Byzantine tradition, Alexius was able to save himself from
being attacked dangerously by more than one enemy
at a time. Pecheneg invasion from the north followed
Norman attack from the west and reached at one
time even to the vicinity of Constantinople itself, but
by 1091 this threat was ended. Improved diplomatic
relations with the papacy seemed possible when
Urban II in 1089 took the initiative in urging a restoration of peace and harmony in the Church, and the
Greeks responded in a friendly spirit. Although none

of the controversial issues were resolved, relations between the emperor and the pope were improved, the
former ceasing to back the Emperor Henry IV and his
antipope and the latter withdrawing support of the
Normans. This easing of relations came at a time when
the Turkish menace to the Byzantine Empire was no
longer desperate and when, instead, Alexius, having
repulsed the enemies on his European frontiers and
consolidated his political position as emperor at Constantinople, felt himself free to plan an offensive against
the Seljuks for the recovery of Asia Minor. In previous
years the emperor had sought to hire fighting men
in the West. At one time he had negotiated with the
papacy for aid in raising recruits against the barbarians
on the Danube. He had persuaded the count of
Flanders, returning about 1090 from a pilgrimage to
Jerusalem, to send him a contingent of fighting men.
The employment of such foreign mercenaries in Byzantine armies was a practice of long standing. It may
be presumed, therefore, that the imperial embassy that
appeared at the Council of Piacenza in 1095 was expecting to negotiate with the papacy in terms of already established imperial policy, without assuming
that Alexius expected Urban to become his chief recruiting agent. The appeal, however, offered an occasion for Pope Urban II to urge upon Western
Christendom the reconquest, not of Asia Minor—the
object of Byzantine ambition—but of the Holy Sepulcher—an object of Western piety. From his exhorta-
tion at Clermont resulted the First Crusade.

The Council of Clermont

For half a century the papacy, directed by reforming
popes such as Leo IX and Gregory VII, had been
striving to achieve a position of moral leadership in
Latin Christendom. With respect to the clergy this
had been achieved through enforcing the canons regarding celibacy and against simony. With respect to

the feudal laity the Church was attempting to put
some curb upon brutal disorder through organizing
the Peace of God and the Truce of God and by trying
to free the clergy from feudal, secular influence. This
last effort had led to the Investiture Struggle, which
was far from settled in 1095. For ten years Emperor
Henry IV had maintained an antipope in Italy, and
in 1095 Urban II did not enjoy safe possession of
Rome itself. The preaching of the crusade, therefore,
can reasonably be considered as part of the general
papal policy of asserting moral leadership and authority
over militant Christianity. It should be recognized that
the first and most successful crusade was a popular
movement from which the kings of Europe held aloof.
The German emperor was excommunicated because of
the Investiture Struggle. The king of France was under
a similar ban for flagrant violation of the marriage
canons. The king of England was using the papal
schism as a possible means of freeing the English
Church from the papacy, refusing to recognize either
Urban II or the emperor's antipope as head of the
Church, and in this he had the support of the English
bishops. In Spain the Almoravide peril absorbed royal
attention. By his successful appeal to popular religious
fervor, Urban gained that position of Christian leadership which befitted the theocratic ideals of the Hilde-
brandine reformers, confounding and embarrassing the
supporters of Emperor Henry and his antipope in Italy.

In November 1095, Pope Urban held a council of
French prelates at Clermont in Auvergne. Most of the
business dealt with ecclesiastical matters, the renewal
of the ban against King Philip of France for his
matrimonial irregularities and further attempts to
establish and extend the Peace and Truce of God.
To these the pope added an eloquent appeal for a
great pilgrimage to recover the Holy Places from the
infidel. It is this novelty and its probably unexpected
results that made the occasion historically important.
In urging the French to undertake a holy war, the

pope dwelt upon the requests for aid that had come from the East, the sufferings of pilgrims and Christians there, and the need for giving assistance against the advancing Muslims. The evil private wars of Christian against Christian, which the Church was trying to curb, should be replaced by this holy war against the infidel, who could not hope to withstand the brave men from the West. The hardships of living in Europe would be exchanged for the pleasures of a land flowing with milk and honey. To those who took the cross, and to their families and property, the Church extended its protection. Within the jurisdiction of the episcopal courts they could gain respite from their debts, while their property, for the period of pilgrimage, would enjoy the same exemption from secular control as did church property. For sinners the expedition offered the chance of plenary indulgence, another novelty.

You, oppressors of orphans and widows; you, murderers and violators of churches; you, robbers of the property of others; you, who, like vultures are drawn to the scent of the battlefield, hasten as you love your souls, under your captain Christ to the rescue of Jerusalem. All you who are guilty of such sins as exclude you from the kingdom of God, ransom yourselves at this price, for such is the will of god!

And "when Pope Urban had said these and very many similar things in his urbane discourse, he so influenced to one purpose the desires of all who were present that they cried out 'God wills it! God wills it!'" Those who vowed themselves to make this pilgrimage were directed to sew white crosses on their shoulders, whence the term crusader (from the verb meaning "to mark with a cross").

The clergy were directed by the pope to preach the crusade in their jurisdictions, while itinerant preachers went about on the same mission. One of these, Peter the Hermit, became a legendary figure of such pro-

portions that he was credited with initiating the whole
movement. Later scholarship exposed this exaggera-
tion and identified Urban as the prime mover. The
pope toured France where he stirred up so much popular enthusiasm that contemporaries felt this could be
explained only as evidence of heavenly assistance. From
the start, Pope Urban assumed general direction of the
movement, appointing Bishop Adhemar of Puy as his
legate to head the expedition. His aim was an army
of fighting men and he warned against admitting the
militarily unfit into the crusading bands. He named
Constantinople as the rendezvous for the pilgrims,
wrote to the Emperor Alexius to provide for them as
they crossed his territory, and undertook to excite the
interest of the naval republics in Italy. Presumably the
local preaching took on the quality of religious revivalism such as even twentieth-century communities
sometimes experienced. In some places in Germany this
found expression in popular outbreaks against the
Jews, resulting in pogroms despite the efforts of local
authorities and ecclesiastics. Possibly the popular response to the crusading idea exceeded papal expectations. The belief that God had inspired the movement
might seem to guarantee success. Furthermore, here
was an opportunity for indulging in warlike adventure
under an ascetic guise, with the possibility of worldly
advantage in a new land and a certainty of spiritual
benefits like those of the martyrs to all eternity. The
fanatic, the adventurer, the enterprising merchant, the
debtor, the serf, and the outlaw, all found in the
crusade a welcome occasion for possible betterment.
While in large measure the rank and file in the
crusading armies were actuated by motives of piety
and genuine religious enthusiasm, the principal leaders, in varying respects, regarded the enterprise as also
an act of political conquest in which they could hope
to carve out principalities for themselves in Syria,
much as their contemporaries had done in England,
Spain, and Sicily. Since for the Byzantine emperor the

Peter the Hermit preaching the First Crusade, 1096. Painting, nineteenth century. (*Three Lions*)

whole movement was presumably related to his ambition to recover territories only recently lost to the Turks, the possibility of a clash of interests between Greeks and crusaders was considerable.

Setting for the First Crusade

The pilgrim character of the early crusades in particular had certain very serious military handicaps, some of which were characteristic of most feudal warfare. In most cases not even the bonds of feudal relationships held the various groups together. Each individual crusader was a pilgrim vowed to visit the Holy Sepulcher, but the time and means of fulfilling his vow was largely at his own discretion. Unless he was the personal retainer of some lord, he was subject to no one's orders, although probably he would attach himself temporarily to the company of some prominent leader. Consequently, there was no real discipline and very little direction. On the First Crusade the chief princes as a group attempted to make decisions, and the papal legate, as long as he was alive, exerted a moral influence. But the leaders were prone to quarrel if their personal ambitions clashed, or to undertake independent enterprises away from the main body. The necessity of living off the country often led to depredations against Christian communities along the line of march, while it enabled the enemy to starve the crusaders by devastating the region through which they must advance. In addition, despite the pope's admonition, there were numerous noncombatants—all pilgrims under vows—who served only to make the march slower and more disorderly and consumed supplies without contributing anything to the work of conquest. Small wonder that the expenditure of effort and life was huge and the immediate results very small.

That the First Crusade did succeed is, in large part, to be explained by the conditions prevailing among

the Muslims of western Asia in the last decade of the
eleventh century. Had the expedition come a generation earlier or later, it probably would have encountered much more effective resistance. The Seljuk principalities in Asia Minor and Syria were mere military
states in which a chief with his band of warriors
imposed his authority and levied tribute upon the mass
of the population. This rule, by its nature, was
superficial and fluctuating. Local wars of conquest,
fraternal rivalries for succession, and usurpations by
military captains produced conditions of chronic political and territorial instability. The conquering union
created and maintained by the first two Seljuk sultans
was less apparent under the third, and disappeared entirely in 1092 when an assassin struck him down. Indeed the appearance at this time of the brotherhood of
the Assassins brought in a new and peculiar agency for
political disorder. This was a Shiite revolutionary organization aiming at the destruction of Seljuk rule
and the overthrow of the Sunnite Caliphate at Bagdad.
Its leader and founder, Hassan Sabbah, established his
headquarters in an impregnable mountain stronghold
in northern Persia and sought to set up similar fortress centers of action throughout Muslim west Asia.
Members of the brotherhood were sworn to unquestion-
ing obedience to the grand prior of the order, popu-
larly known in later years as "The Old Man of the
Mountain." Stimulated by religious fervor, assisted
supposedly by the use of hashish, these fanatics carried on a new form of holy war by systematized assassination of political leaders. Since this must be done
by direct attack with a dagger, each assassin expected to
die a martyr's death himself in performing his office.
Sultans, caliphs, viziers, and emirs were their victims,
while the uncertainties and discords of Muslim politics,
largely a matter of personal factions, were accentuated
by this new and incalculable terror. Furthermore, it
will be recalled that Syria, the objective of the crusading
army, had been a bone of contention between the Sun-

nite Turks and the Shiite Egyptians. Each willingly saw the other beaten by the Christians. While the latter defeated the Turkish emirs in northern Syria, the Egyptians drove the Turks out of Jerusalem. When the crusaders turned to take that city, there was no assistance from the neighboring Sunnite states. Throughout the First Crusade the crusaders met with only local resistance. The opposition from Egypt might have been more formidable had not the caliphs at Cairo felt themselves threatened from the west by Yusuf ibn-Tashfin and the Almoravides, who, in addition to their conquest of Spain, were aiming to conquer Tunis, a tributary to Cairo and the region from which the Fatimids themselves had moved to the conquest of Egypt. To the Egyptians this appeared to be a much greater danger than the crusaders. Indeed, from the Muslim point of view, the crusades were episodes of merely local significance.

In the fall of 1096 the principal crusading armies arrived successively at Constantinople. Generally speaking, there were three groups: the Lotharingians from the Rhinelands, among whom the most prominent leader was Godfrey of Bouillon, Duke of Lower Lorraine; the Provençals from southern France under Raymond of St. Gilles, Count of Toulouse; and the Normans from southern Italy led by Bohemund with his nephew Tancred. They had been preceded by an ill-organized crowd of pilgrims, the so-called Peasants' Crusade, enthusiastic folk led by Peter the Hermit—who believed that their efforts were indeed according to God's will and therefore could not fail. Shortly after these peasants passed over into Asia Minor, they were massacred by the Turks. When the fighting men arrived on the Bosporus, one of the fundamental difficulties of the whole crusading movement immediately appeared, namely, the relations of the Westerners to the Byzantine emperor. Alexius Comnenus and his successors were quite devoid of that religious ardor which presumably actuated the crusaders. The em-

peror looked to recover Asia Minor and to defend his
frontiers against attack from the east. His predecessors
had hired fighting forces from the West for similar
military purposes, although never in such numbers
nor under such important leaders. These Western leaders from the start no doubt expected to join with the
Byzantines in expelling the Turks from western Asia,
but they had personal ambitions as well, similar in
a general way to what other anti-Muslim fighters had
achieved for themselves in Spain and Sicily. These
ambitions ran counter to imperial policy and were
of a sort to lead, on occasion, to open hostility with
their imperial ally. They wanted to conquer principalities for themselves in Syria, or in any other
place where conquest might be effected. "In appearance," wrote Anna Comnena, her father's biographer,
"they were on a pilgrimage to Jerusalem, but in truth
they wanted to oust the Emperor from his throne and
to seize the capital." The presence of the Norman leaders gave some reasonable color to this suspicion. It
seems possible that papal policy included a hope that
the crusade might help to bring together again the
Western and Eastern churches, but for many crusaders
we may suspect that the Greeks were regarded with
hostility as schismatics. The mutual antipathy of the
cultured and the barbarous and the presence in the
crusading host of Bohemund and his Normans, old
and formidable enemies of the empire, made for friction, suspicion, and fear on both sides. Difficulties
were smoothed over temporarily when the crusading
chiefs did homage to the emperor. The latter promised
to take the cross and to bring reinforcements to the
Latin armies. But the clash of interests remained in
the Byzantine ambition to exercise suzerainty over
crusading princes who might establish themselves in
territory formerly Byzantine and the desire of the
latter to be independent. This rivalry was accentuated
by the old Norman ambition to conquer the Byzantine
Empire.

The First Crusade

The campaign began in the spring of 1097 with a successful siege of Nicaea, but the Greeks thwarted the Latin expectations of sacking the city. A pitched battle on August 1 at Dorylaeum opened the road across Asia Minor to the crusaders, but the devastated condition of the country caused them frightful losses as they advanced, particularly in horses, a very serious matter for an army of knights. With the passage of the Taurus Mountains, the real purpose of some of the leaders became apparent; certain of them began making local conquests for themselves, quarreling with each other for the possession of cities, and turning aside from the main expedition's line of march. Notable among these personal ventures was one by Baldwin, the younger brother of Duke Godfrey, to the Armenian city of Edessa, a Christian community with a Christian ruler, located in Mesopotamia east of the Euphrates. Entering the service of this prince, Baldwin was adopted by him as his heir. A local revolution soon followed. The Armenian ruler was killed, and Baldwin ruled in his stead, marrying an Armenian princess and leaving the conquest of Jerusalem to others. We will hear of Baldwin again.

Meanwhile the main body of crusaders moved on into Syria and laid siege to Antioch in October 1097. Here contact with the sea made possible more effective supply, and from this point the fleets of the Italian republics became very essential factors, bringing supplies and providing siege engines for use against Antioch's formidable fortifications. The city would not have been taken, however, had it not been for local malcontents within who arranged with Bohemund to admit his Normans inside the walls on June 3, 1098. Three days later a Turkish army under the emir of Mosul came to relieve Antioch and besieged the Latins in their turn in the newly captured city. Fortunately for the Christians, the Muslim chiefs were mutually

hostile to each other and little disposed to fight under
an unpopular commander. While the beleaguered
crusaders were desperate, a poor man in the following of Raymond of St. Gilles declared that St. Andrew
had appeared to him in a dream and revealed the
whereabouts of the lance that had pierced Christ on
the cross, an unusually potent relic. The papal legate
was skeptical, but Count Raymond believed the man.
Day-long digging produced nothing, but when the
dreamer leaped into the pit he at once found a piece
of iron, which was taken to be a lance head. As a
result of this miraculous evidence of divine support
the army turned from a state of depression to one
of enthusiasm. In this elevated frame of mind, led into
the field by Bohemund, their most skillful military
leader, the crusaders sortied from Antioch on June 28,
1098, and won an apparently miraculous victory.

But with success the rivalries among the crusading
chiefs became more bitter. Bohemund and Raymond
disputed angrily for the possession of Antioch. Their
dissension delayed further advance until the following
year, during which the Egyptians occupied Jerusalem.
Even then it was the clamor of the rank and file, for
whom the crusade was primarily a pilgrimage in ful-
fillment of their vows, which forced Godfrey and
Raymond to leave Antioch to Bohemund and to move
on to the Holy City. Arriving before the walls on
June 6, 1099, they took the place by storm on the
fifteenth. "And if you desire to know what was done
with the enemy who were found there," wrote one
prince to his wife, "know that in Solomon's Porch
and in his temple our men rode in the blood of
the Saracens up to the knees of their horses." Two
months later this conquest was assured by the de-
moralizing defeat of an Egyptian army near Ascalon.
The capture of that city was prevented by a quarrel
between Godfrey and Raymond as to which of them
should have it. The count of Toulouse, disappointed
for the second time, set about winning territory for

himself on the coast around the city of Tripoli. That place was taken in 1109, but Raymond had died four years before.

The Latin Kingdom of Jerusalem

For the pilgrims on the First Crusade, those who survived to the end, the expedition had been a great success. They had triumphantly accomplished their vows, defeated and killed infidels, prayed at the Holy Sepulcher, bathed in the Jordan. They could now return home justified, and most of them did so. For the adventurers, for whom the expedition was a more practical matter, the difficulties were not yet over. How to retain the Holy City rescued from the Muslims was not an easy matter. The conquest of Palestine and the Syrian coast was only begun. Their extraordinary success seemed to prove that God approved their venture. They were filled with confidence which led to the formulation of plans for the conquest of Egypt. These were never accomplished, but they were repeatedly revived throughout the whole crusading epoch. When we consider how extraordinary was the success of the First Crusade, the only really successful crusade, we may perhaps be justified in speculating on the probable consequences had it failed, as it well might have done. It seems unlikely in that case that such an effort would have been made again. The energies of Western Europe, which were expended in repeated attempts to protect or rescue the fruits of victory won in 1099, would presumably have been otherwise employed, whether for better or for worse no one can say.

The newly conquered lands had to be organized. The original plan was for an ecclesiastical state in which the secular princes did homage to the patriarch of Jerusalem to whom, of course, the pope was superior. It was in this connection that Godfrey of Bouillon was chosen, not king, but "Advocate of the Church of

the Holy Sepulcher" *(Advocatus Sancti Sepulchri),* a
title intended to indicate the authority necessary for
defending the holy place. Almost immediately the pre-
cariousness of the Latin position in the East became
apparent. Within a year of the capture of Jerusalem
Godfrey was dead, and Bohemund, Prince of Antioch,
had been captured to be held a prisoner for ransom
for three years in a Turkish castle. In the following
year (1101), three new armies coming from Europe to
reinforce the crusaders and carry on the holy war, after
enduring great suffering in Asia Minor from thirst
and famine, were dispersed and massacred by the
Turks.

The real founder of the Latin Kingdom of Jerusalem
was Godfrey's younger brother Baldwin of Edessa, the
crusading leader who had been so occupied with his
own interests that he had taken no part in the capture
of Antioch and Jerusalem. Less religious but more
statesmanlike, as well as more self-seeking, than his
brother, Baldwin transformed the ecclesiastical principality into a feudal kingdom, assumed the title
"King of Jerusalem," and labored with some success
to effect and maintain a sort of political and military
unity among the Christian leaders. With an eye to
practical realities he undertook to strengthen the
Frankish position by conciliating the local population
irrespective of religion and by making alliances with
the Italian city-republics that could provide naval
power. The continuous assistance of the latter was
essential, for the capture of the Syrian coast towns,
for resistance to the Egyptian fleets, and for assuring
communications with, and supplies from, Europe. In
seeking agreements with the Venetians, Godfrey had
already found that they put a high price on their
assistance. Their standard of value was the privileges
that they already enjoyed at Constantinople. Their
interest in crusading was free from inhibiting religious
sentiment. King Baldwin and the other Latin princes
turned to the Genoese and Pisans who, however, viewed

the situation much like the Venetians. In general, the naval republics demanded and gained, in addition to their share of the booty, special quarters in captured coastal cities—usually one third of the area—which would be directly under the jurisdiction of the Italian city-state. We can see here an early form of extra-territoriality. More significant still were the rights of importing and selling goods in the crusader states without paying taxes. With these advantages, Italian commercial colonies grew up in the Latin Kingdom not subject to the royal government. They monopolized trade and absorbed the revenues of the ports, upon whose activities the economic life of the kingdom depended. Such an arrangement stimulated commerce without increasing the revenues of the crusader states and the viability of those states was always precarious. From the start the material interests of the Italian merchants became a decisive factor in the history of the Latin Kingdom. The Christian conquest of the Syrian coast, completed in 1124 by the surrender of Tyre, served to establish the Italian position there. Continued Christian rule of that region, however, would not be necessary for carrying on a profitable commerce by the Italians if merchants could make satisfactory arrangements later with the Muslims, particularly the Egyptians.

It was unfortunate that the crusaders in Syria did not maintain satisfactory relations with the Byzantine emperor. Large measure of blame for this lies with Bohemund and the Normans in Antioch. In appropriating that city, Bohemund repudiated his earlier oath to Alexius and resumed an attitude of aggressive hostility both to the north and on the coast. Possibilities of Byzantine military and naval help in the conquest of Syria, and hopes for steps toward reconciliation between the churches went glimmering. Alexius had recovered the coast of Asia Minor, but Turkish resistance farther inland now had encouragement and even help from Bohemund. The latter and Tancred, his nephew

and lieutenant, were equally aggressive toward their
fellow crusaders as well as toward the adjacent Turks—
all of which alarmed and alienated their neighbors.
For a short time the Normans were riding high, but
a disastrous battle with the emirs of Mosul and Mardin
so endangered Bohemund's position that he returned to
Italy. Here he undertook to recoup his fortunes by
a new attack on the Byzantine Empire in Albania.
To justify this he aimed to capitalize on the anti-
Byzantine sentiment stemming from recent events,
along with his own prestige as the hero of the First
Crusade. The treacherous actions of the perfidious
Greeks were responsible, he said, for all the crusaders'
disasters. Pope Urban's successor was persuaded to
sanction a new "crusade" in 1106, which was to be
in fact a Norman attack on the Byzantines, launched
the following year. Alexius, however, was adequately
prepared and the invaders were not only held at the
coast but were forced to come to terms. From this
reverse Bohemund never recovered; he died in 1111.
Nonetheless, his anti-Byzantine propaganda contributed
considerably to Western hostility toward the Greeks,
and the linking of the idea of crusading with that
hostility became significant in later years.

The most important result of the First Crusade was
the establishment of a new point of contact between
East and West in a region that had unusual religious
and commercial attractions for the Latin Christians
of Europe. The leaders of the First Crusade had been
moved to participate in that expedition, not only by
religious motives, but also by the desire to gain for
themselves principalities in a land reputed to be rich
and prosperous. Consequently, the period of the first
generation of crusaders, roughly to about 1124, was
one of continued warfare for the establishment of four
Latin states; the county of Edessa, a frontier area in
the upper Euphrates valley, the principality of Antioch
in northern Syria, the county of Tripoli on the coast,
and the kingdom of Jerusalem facing the Egyptians

in the south. Their chief local opponents were the
emirs of Aleppo and Damascus on the east, and the
caliph of Cairo in the south. The military strength of
the Christian states was limited, and the country was
never completely subdued. Consequently, the second
generation of Frankish rulers—heirs and successors to
the men of the First Crusade—preferred, when possible, a policy of conciliation although apparent opportunities for local conquests were welcomed. The
personal feuds and jealousies that kept the Muslim
rulers at odds with each other helped the crusaders.
The latter found themselves a small organized fighting class ruling over a large alien population, sub-
missive but of uncertain loyalty, differing from them
in customs, language, and religion, but upon whom
they were dependent for subsistence. In this respect
their position was analogous to that of the Turkish
military chiefs whom they replaced, although the cultural and religious gap between the Christian ruler
and his native subjects was probably greater. Furthermore, the Latins soon discovered that much was to be
gained by trade with the adjacent Muslims, and the
latter were not unresponsive. The fanatical spirit that
had actuated the original pilgrim host, the force which
captured Jerusalem, declined among the Europeans
who settled in Syria, although the habitual warlike
activities characteristic of feudal society persisted.
Border fighting was intermittent and persistent, and
sometimes the Latins suffered serious defeats in battle.
But the Latin rulers did not hesitate to form alliances
with Muslim emirs against their Christian rivals, and
the emirs were equally free from religious prejudice.
In general, the relations of Frankish lords with neighboring Muslim rulers were, at times, almost as friendly, although not as stable, as with the other Christian
barons of the kingdom. Among the fighting men, Christians and Muslims learned to respect each other with
the result that, through constant intercourse, the Christians learned in detail the more cultivated manner of

living that prevailed among the Muslims. The fanaticism of the holy war was mitigated by a certain tolerant cosmopolitanism and a political realism that shocked Westerners newly come to the Holy Land. The Latins sometimes intermarried with Armenians and Christian Syrians. They struck coins with Arabic inscriptions, even with quotations from the Koran, in order to facilitate trade. The native farmers and Arab merchants were well treated by the Christian rulers, and Muslims worshipped publicly without fear of molestation.

Pilgrims and the Military Orders

It was not the Latins who settled in Syria, however, who played the role of unconscious civilizing agents for western Europe. They merely provided a connection whereby their fellow Christians from home were able to discover the East with its different and more cultivated way of life. The recovery of the Holy Places, and the recurrent necessity of attempting their defense, greatly stimulated travel from Europe to Syria. Pilgrims by thousands visited the Holy Land and then, after a longer or shorter sojourn there, returned home, bringing back novelties learned overseas, having developed the larger point of view that comes with travel and from contact with a different and superior civilization. Presumably the prestige enjoyed by returned palmers lent weight to their reports. Pilgrim transport became an important and profitable business that suggests something of the nineteenth-century shipment of emigrants from Europe to America and the twentieth-century tourist trade of Americans going to Europe. Large vessels, specially built for this traffic, sailed regularly from the ports of Italy and southern France at Easter and in June, carrying pilgrims to Syria. When we consider that this continued, intermittently no doubt, for upward of a century and a half, we get the impression of a movement of peoples to and fro of very large proportions. Periodically, too, when the

Latin Kingdom was threatened, great expeditions, which naturally loom large in contemporary accounts and so assume an appearance of importance in the history of the crusades that can be overemphasized, would be organized to bring assistance to the eastern Christians. These organized efforts would temporarily increase the number of those going to the East, but presumably most of these crusaders, if they survived, returned to Europe when the emergency had passed. Continually, the Levantine principalities were needing and seeking recruits and reinforcements in the West, and younger sons and military adventurers were going out to seek their fortunes in Syria.

It is the situation produced by this stream of pilgrims from Europe, needing help in various forms, and the persistent military weakness of the Latin Kingdom that brought into existence the military orders, those chiv-alric-ascetic organizations of fighting men peculiar to the crusading movement. These were religious congregations of soldier-monks, bound by the monastic vows of poverty, chastity, and obedience, devoted to the care and defense of pilgrims, and imbued with ardor for war for the faith. In them the true spirit of crusading tended to persist longer than in other settlers. When the crusaders captured Jerusalem, they found there a hospital for pilgrims built by merchants of Amalfi in 1070 and dedicated to St. John. Favored by the first two Latin kings, it continued to function as an institution devoted to the sick. With the choice in 1120 of Raymond du Puy as its head, its wealth grew and its character changed. By making gifts to the hospital, pious persons in Europe could support the crusade without making the long journey to Jerusalem, and this enthusiasm enabled Raymond, when touring the West, to enrich his organization on a large scale. He also added military duties to those of tending the sick, and the Knights of St. John of Jerusalem (Hospitalers) are his creation. At the same time Hugh de Payens in 1119 formed the first band of knights for defending pilgrims on their journey. According to St. Bernard, by seeking recruits among excommunicated knights this organization turned "rogues and impious men, robbers and committers of sacrilege, murderers, perjurers and adulterers" into ardent soldiers of the cross. With the backing of St. Bernard, the Order of Knights Templar was sanctioned in 1128. Composed in considerable measure of nobles who had renounced their worldly interests at home without seeking new fiefs in Syria, these orders formed a permanent fighting force in the East where they maintained the spirit of an unflagging holy war not always wisely. Saladin regarded them as implacable enemies to be ruthlessly destroyed whenever possible. Becoming popular in the West, their numbers increased, their chapters multiplied throughout Europe, popes conferred privileges upon them including immunity from secular ecclesiastical authority, and they became rich and powerful. In this way they became one of the important links between Europe and Syria, active agents in stimulating and supporting pilgrim activities, particularly in matters of finance, and in transmitting Oriental cultural influences.

The Loss of Edessa

As experiments in colonization, the Latin principalities established by the crusaders were failures, and in that fact may be found an explanation for the eventual cessation of crusading to the Levant. We have already noted that the number of permanent settlers was relatively small. In addition, the political life of the community tended to be one of intermittent crisis, both internal and external. Muslim hostility toward the crusaders was confused and limited by the rivalry between the emirs of Aleppo and Damascus and their concern lest they be subjugated by Muslim rulers farther east in Mosul and Bagdad. This last seemed more menacing than the Latins. Political activities of the Assassins, who established castles in Syria, added to the confusion. Combined action of these emirs with Egypt was inhibited, but not always prevented, by sectarian religious hostility. The continued existence of the crusader states depended on the persistence of these divisions and dissensions among their Muslim neighbors. Should these unite effectively, the Christians would be surrounded. As it was, the county of Edessa in the northeast was in an exposed position inviting attack from farther east. Aleppo on the Muslim side was similarly isolated and excited Latin ambitions from Edessa and Antioch.

A new chapter in crusading history opens in 1127 when the Seljuk sultan at Bagdad appointed as atabeg of Mosul a certain Zengi, who was to prove himself a ruthless, tyrannous, competent ruler ambitious to use his position to create for himself a large hereditary principality. His first step was to confirm and so perpetuate a union of Mosul and Aleppo, and with this foundation to extend his power and territory in any direction where opportunity offered. Most of his efforts were directed against his Muslim neighbors to the north and east. Once he attempted to seize Bagdad itself. Damascus and Edessa were possible objects of his ambitions. He hoped to use the call to a holy war against the Christians as a means of gaining control over Damascus but the people of that city feared Zengi's rule and resisted his efforts, preferring an alliance with the king of Jerusalem. Other local emirs also sought assistance from the crusaders, and at a call from one of these the count of Edessa led his forces away from the city. Learning that Edessa was temporarily weakened, Zengi made a sudden attack and took it by storm, December 24, 1144, before the count could bring relief. All the Franks in the city were massacred and the Latin churches destroyed, but the Armenian Christians were spared, only to be destroyed two years later by Zengi's successor. This victory made Zengi appear the champion of Islam against the Christians. For him it offered occasion for attacking Damascus and subduing other Muslim allies of the crusaders, but while so engaged he was assassinated. That his territories did not fall apart at this event was due to the capacity of his second son Nureddin who succeeded him.

The Second Crusade

In the course of 1145, news of the loss of Edessa reached the West with appeals for help from Armenian bishops and from Antioch and Jerusalem. In December, Pope Eugenius III issued a bull calling for a new crusade, the first of its kind, setting forth the privileges to be enjoyed by crusaders. It indicates clearly the papal assumption of official leadership of the crusading movement. At the same time King Louis VII of France announced his desire to go to the help of the Eastern Christians. A few months later, at Vezelay, the king and St. Bernard the abbot of Clairvaux, launched the crusade before an enthusiastic gathering of the French nobility. During a year of preparation Bernard preached the crusade in France and Germany. Again religious revivalism stirred up outbreaks of anti-semitism despite Bernard's denunciation. In Germany, Emperor Conrad III was very reluctant to take the cross, nor was the pope eager to have him do so, but Bernard's repeated enthusiastic exhortations eventually persuaded him, a result that even the saint regarded as miraculous. This meant that the second Crusade, led by the two chief Western monarchs, would be a better organized expedition than its predecessor. Another novel feature was the frank papal recognition that the virtues and benefits of crusading were extendable to other areas, where pious warriors could fight for the faith against Muslims in Spain and North Africa, or against the pagan Wends in Pomerania. The logic of this in terms of the holy war will be apparer.t, but the possible future distraction from the fighting in Syria is obvious.

In so extending crusader privileges, the pope merely recognized that the expeditions to Syria had not turned Christian Europe away from continuing to combat the Muslims at the older points of contact. The immediate successor to Urban II preached a crusade against the Moorish pirates who occupied the Balearic islands, and the counts of Catalonia in alliance with the Pisans made temporary conquest of some of these in 1114–1115. The Genoese fleets similarly helped the kings of Castile to capture cities on the coast of Spain. Roger II, the Norman ruler of Sicily, looked aggressively southward to the North African shore and in 1118 launched a campaign of conquest against Tunis which lasted nine years. Broken off at that time because of more pressing matters in Italy, it was renewed in 1134, and the whole coast from Bona to Tripoli temporarily subjugated. One of the features of the Second Crusade appears in the action of a band of crusaders from northern Europe who were faring by sea and who stopped on the west coast of the Iberian peninsula to help the Portuguese capture Lisbon in 1147. This was one of the few permanent results of that great effort known as the Second Crusade.

As before, the German and French crusading armies rendezvoused at Constantinople and moved from there successively into Asia Minor. In each army there were aggressive elements who vainly urged the German emperor and the French king to turn their forces against the Byzantines. Roger of Sicily saw in the Byzantine emperor's unavoidable preoccupation with the crusaders an opportunity for renewed Norman attacks in Albania and Greece. The formidable strength of the Second Crusade was dissipated in the attempt to advance through Asia Minor, where the harassing attacks of the Turks and the difficulties of supply proved disastrous. When remnants of the two armies did reach Syria, instead of attempting to recover Edessa, whose loss had brought about the crusade, the two European monarchs were persuaded to join the men of the Latin Kingdom to attack Damascus, one of the important Muslim principalities on the kingdom's eastern frontier. The effort was a dismal failure. It marks the end of the Second Crusade. As a result of all this, the Westerners became suspicious and hostile toward the Latin Christians in the East. These latter they found living like Muslims, and apparently no longer imbued with the religious fanaticism and earnestness that had achieved victory in 1099. The survivors of the Second Crusade reported bitterly that their failure to capture Damascus was due to the defection of the men of Jerusalem corrupted by Muslim gold, but they added with satisfaction that the gold proved to be nothing but gilded brass. The ability and willingness of Western Christendom to provide adequate support to the crusader states could well be questioned.

Weakness of the Latin Kingdom

The Latin Kingdom itself was as weakly organized as can be imagined. Instead of being a united state, it consisted of four principalities bound together by very loose feudal bonds, with ambitious rulers prone to quarrel among themselves and not unwilling to prey upon each other. In this respect, of course, they merely reflected the characteristics of Western feudal society minus an accepted, traditional, feudal king such as the king of France. We have noted how important sources of revenue were denied the crusading states because of the privileged Italian commercial monopolies. Disunion was accentuated by the trade rivalries of the Italian republics with each other. This not only injected their feuds into Syrian politics but, on occasion, led them to discover that agreements with the Muslims could be more profitable than with their fellow Christians. The Hospitalers and Templars, upon whom the kingdom depended for a considerable, permanent fighting force, became antagonistic to each other. This enmity added to the military and political confusion. The exertions of conquest and defense in an unaccustomed climate seems to have worn out the ruling race, which tended to die off more rapidly than in the West. King Baldwin IV became a leper and died at the age of twenty-four. This reduced life span meant frequent minorities in each of the crusading states, often under the regencies of women. Eventually a disputed succession to the throne of Jerusalem completed the disorganization of the kingdom. Furthermore, the persistent efforts of the Byzantine emperors to force their suzerainty upon the Latin princes diverted the latter on occasion from the Muslim war to no good purpose. The Byzantines were not themselves prepared to wage a first-class war against the infidel, and they were not strong enough to protect the Latin Kingdom from a vigorous Muslim attack. The preservation of that kingdom was not, in fact, a vital interest of any strong European state, nor was the kingdom itself a viable state. Its continued existence depended on the weakness of the Muslims rather than the strength of the Christians. The Latins conquered scarcely more than the coast of Syria. They were always exposed on the east to such Muslim states as Mosul, Aleppo, and Damascus, and on the south to the Egyptians. Yet it should be remarked that, considering the kaleidoscopic history of most Levantine principalities, a state that could last for two centuries was unusual, even if international exertions on a large scale were occasionally required.

As long as the Turkish emirs of western Asia fought among themselves, the Latin Kingdom could be maintained by its own efforts with some success. By alliances and truces with rival emirs the Latin princes contributed to Muslim disunion and themselves cherished territorial ambitions even that of a possible conquest of Egypt. As long as the Muslims quarreled and were concerned with threats from farther east, the danger of an attack upon the crusader states in sufficient strength to threaten their existence was not pressing.

With the exception of the Hospitalers and the Templars, the ardor for fighting a holy war was considerably abated on both sides. If a ruler should appear who could unite the Muslims under a single effective rule with some prospect of continuity and stability, the recovery of Syria was certain to be attempted. If in addition some enthusiasm for a jihad, a war for the faith against the unbeliever, could be aroused, an element of persistence and purposeful idealism would give added strength to the Muslim effort. Such a situation arose with the career of Zengi, atabeg of Mosul, who took Aleppo from his Muslim rivals and Edessa from the crusaders. An important and unusual development not often encountered in Muslim history arose from the fact that Zengi's son and successor, Nureddin, was as competent and fortunate as his father, and was himself followed by an even more able leader. In consequence, Zengi's territories, instead of falling apart and becoming again the holdings of ambitious rivals, were kept united although not without considerable effort, which distracted attention from the crusaders in Syria. But Nureddin secured Damascus, and when the last Fatimid caliph in Cairo died in 1171, he intervened successfully in Egypt. This not only encircled the Christian states but it eliminated the sectarian rivalry between Sunnite Abassids and Shiitie Fatimids that had been so helpful to the first crusaders in 1099. Furthermore, Nureddin inaugurated a religious revival among the Muslims of his territories, not the fanatical revivalism of the Almoravide type, but a serious cultural effort that made a popular appeal and gave new vigor to the idea of a holy war.

Saladin's Conquest of Jerusalem

When Nureddin died in 1174, his son was a minor. His real successor was his lieutenant Saladin, then governing Egypt. A distinguished modern scholar writes:

. . . the reign of Saladin is more than an episode in the history of the Crusades. It is one of those rare and dramatic moments in human history when cynicism and disillusion born of long experience of the selfish ambitions of princes, are for a brief period dislodged by moral determination and unity of purpose. . . . For a brief but decisive moment, by sheer goodness and firmness of character, he raised Islam out of the rut of political demoralization. By standing out for a moral ideal and expressing that ideal in his own life and action he created around him an impulse to unity, which, though never quite complete, sufficed to meet the unforeseen challenge flung down to him by destiny.

Since at the start, to many of Nureddin's supporters, Saladin appeared to be a usurper, it took him a decade to make his rule over Nureddin's territories effective. Unlike most Muslim emirs, he aimed at much more than personal aggrandizement. A religious revival under the caliph as Muhammad's successor, uniting the Muslim states and renewing a war for the faith against the Christians in Syria, was his objective. Jerusalem was a sacred city for Muslims as well as Christians. Therein stood the throne of David and the temple of Solomon, there the prophet Muhammad had miraculously ascended into Heaven, and there all men would be gathered together on the Resurrection Day. For an ambitious and dedicated ruler like Saladin, who regarded himself as an instrument of God, the launching of a holy war was a duty. He was statesman enough, however, to hold his hand until he was strong and the Christians were weak. A few Christians, especially those newly come to the East, still burned with the desire to war indiscriminately on the enemies of their religion, and the members of the military orders shared this feeling. For such as these no agreement made with Muslims and no oath given to them was binding, since no faith need be kept with infidels, who are God's enemies. For certain adventurers, too, war against the

Muslims was a means of livelihood. One of the most enterprising had the boldness to build and launch ships on the Red Sea to raid the Egyptian trade routes there, and to attempt an attack on the Muslim Holy Places at Mecca. Truce-breaking and plundering along the caravan road from Cairo to Damascus on the part of irrepressible Christians was common enough to provide Saladin with an excuse for starting his war of reconquest as soon as he was ready.

For a decade the Kingdom of Jerusalem had been torn with factions among the barons competing for control of the kingdom under weak kings. The native barons advocated a defensive policy against Saladin. Certain newcomers, notably Guy of Lusignan, and some restless nobles backed by the military orders opposed this position. Mutual jealousies and personal enmities complicated matters. The possibility of civil war was real, particularly when, on the death of the child king, Baldwin V, Guy of Lusignan was crowned king by a *coup d'état.* When one of Guy's chief supporters wantonly broke a truce with Saladin the latter proclaimed a jihad and attacked. The crusader leaders chose to take the risk of a pitched battle. Faulty leadership made the battle of Hattin, July 4, 1187, an overwhelming disaster for the Christians. Their army was annihilated. King Guy and most of the other Latin leaders were taken prisoner. The True Cross, the most precious of all Christian relics, was captured by the Muslims. It had been brought along with the army as a help toward victory, but the success of the Holy Lance at Antioch in 1098 was not repeated. With his own hand Saladin beheaded the truce-breaker whose actions had brought on the war. It had been his practice even before this to strike off the heads of Templars and Hospitalers taken prisoner. By rapid action Saladin conquered most of the Christian territory, including Jerusalem, in three months. A few places, notably Tyre on the coast, held out. Latin rule in the Holy Land ended. The Byzantine emperor congratulated Saladin and suggested that they form an alliance against the Latins.

The Third Crusade

Although the news from Palestine alarmed Western Christendom, preparations for a Third Crusade could not be effected for two or three years. The first to respond was the aged Emperor Frederick Barbarossa, a veteran of the Second Crusade, a heroic figure in a chivalric age, and a more ardent crusader than his predecessor Conrad. Under him was an unusually large and efficient army. With some difficulty, papal mediation brought about peace between the kings of France and England preliminary to their also taking the cross. If both went to the East, neither would be disadvantaged in Europe. King Philip Augustus and King Richard the Lion-Hearted were very different types. The one was politically calculating and unscrupulous, the other a bold, skillful, adventurous fighter whose qualities appealed to the sentiments of a feudal nobility, but whose understanding of political realities was inferior to Philip's. Contemporaries were impressed with Richard. Modern historians credit Philip with more lasting achievements. The German army proceeded by way of Constantinople into Asia Minor, across which it fought its way much more effectively than during the Second Crusade. Alarmed at the advance of such a formidable force, Saladin summoned all the faithful to meet the danger. When news came that Frederick had been accidentally drowned in a river near Seleucia (June 10, 1190), the Muslims hailed the event as a miraculous sign of God's favor. The Germans became demoralized. Some went home; others took ship for Tyre. A somewhat battered remnant pushed on by land to Antioch and later to Tyre.

Saladin's conquering advance had been stopped by the walls of Tyre. The defense of this port was the first effective Christian resistance after the battle of

Hattin. This was made possible, in considerable part, by the prompt arrival of modest reinforcements from the Norman ruler of Sicily and by the vigorous leadership of a recent newcomer from the West, Conrad of Montferrat. Around him the remnant of the kingdom's nobility gathered. In July 1188 Saladin had generously released King Guy on the latter's taking oath that he would return to Europe and not again fight the Muslims. This promise he soon repudiated with clerical sanction. Guy's return to the crusaders' camp revived with increased vigor the factional animosities that had contributed so much to the earlier disaster. Conrad and the defenders of Tyre refused to accept Guy as king. The latter, to reassert his position, rashly undertook to besiege Acre only to find himself later, even when joined by Conrad, besieged in turn by Saladin. For nearly two years the two forces faced each other in a sort of starving match with some fighting, the Christians unable to take the city, and Saladin unable to bring relief or to raise the siege. Eventually the French and English forces arrived by sea.

Although it was three years after the battle of Hattin before the French and English armies started for Palestine, the two kings showed no impatience to get to their destination. To avoid a winter crossing they wintered in Sicily and became entangled in the politics of the succession to the throne of the Norman kingdom. The French got to Acre in April 1191, but very bad weather caused Richard to land in Cyprus in May. A Byzantine rebel had been ruling Cyprus for five years, calling himself emperor and tyrannizing over the Cypriots. When the English expedition reached Cyprus and the chief crusader leaders crossed over to the island from Acre to confer with Richard, it was decided to conquer Cyprus. By the end of May this was accomplished. The island was part of the Byzantine Empire. Its conquerors made no pretense of fighting infidels, although its strategic value for crusading operations was recognized. Ironically, this conquest was the most lasting of the meager results of the Third Crusade. The siege of Acre could now be pushed and all efforts by Saladin to relieve the city repulsed. On July 12, 1191, the city surrendered. It would remain the chief part of the remnant of the crusader kingdom for a century.

At this point, on plea of ill health, King Philip returned to France. A large part of the French army remained at Acre. Both kings had become involved in the factional politics of the crusader state, Philip favoring Conrad and backed by the Genoese, Richard and the Pisans supporting Guy. Soon after, Duke Leopold of Austria, who had succeeded Frederick Barbarossa as head of the Germans, also departed, infuriated because Richard refused to treat him as an equal. Now in chief command, Richard planned to advance to Jerusalem. First he massacred the Saracen prisoners taken at Acre, and then he marched south. Saladin's forces harassed the crusading army on the march, but when the sultan was emboldened to attack Richard at Arsuf (September 7, 1191), he was repulsed. But the Muslim army still held the field in defense of Jerusalem. This proved decisive. Its presence, undefeated, discouraged Richard from pushing inland to the Holy City lest he be cut off from his supplies coming by sea. When he did approach to within a few miles of Jerusalem, he feared that should he capture the city he would be besieged there with no relief available. For a year fighting along the coast alternated with negotiations between Richard and Saladin. These terminated in a treaty which left Jerusalem in Muslim hands, with permission for Christians to visit the Holy Places, while the crusaders held the coast as far south as Jaffa. The barons of the kingdom forced the recognition of Conrad as king only to have him assassinated within a few days. His widow then married Henry of Champagne, who was accepted as king, while Guy bought Cyprus from Richard and enjoyed a royal status there. In a few years the vagaries of hereditary succession made possible a union of the two crowns, and the kings of Jerusalem continued to reign in Cyprus long after the last crusader city in Syria had been lost. Having learned of the intrigues in England of his younger brother John, Richard was impatient to go home and left the Holy Land in October 1192. Saladin had successfully repulsed the formidable aggregation of power brought together by the greatest European kings. His ability to hold together the Muslim forces and to imbue them with some of his own moral determination had turned the tide in Palestine in Islam's favor. Despite the Third Crusade's show of power, the Christians in Syria never recovered from their earlier defeats. They clung to Acre and some of the other ports, but their retention of these after the departure of the Western armies was due largely to the dissension that developed among Saladin's heirs after his death in March 1193.

C H A P T E R . . . 3

Later Crusades

Christian Successes in Spain and Prussia

It should not be supposed that the expeditions to Syria
distracted Christian Europe from continuing to combat
the Muslims at the other points of contact. As we have
seen, the pope in launching the Second Crusade recognized crusading in Spain and on the eastern frontiers
of Germany as worthy of crusading privileges. Although
in the twelfth century the expeditions against the pagan
Wends in the north had not been particularly successful, the situation in Spain looked more promising. The
Almoravide empire had degenerated into that condition
of anarchy that seems to be the usual fate of Oriental
states, and the ultimate Christian victory over western
Islam appeared imminent. It was delayed, however, by
another fanatical religious revival among the Berbers
stimulated by a new sect, the Almohades. Formed in
Morocco, this new group, under skillful leaders, between 1130 and 1163 conquered North Africa from the
Almoravides and eventually regained for Islam the

recent Norman conquests along the coast. Like their predecessors, the Almohades crossed northward into Spain, and once again united the Iberian Muslims. The result was a cultural and military revival, brilliant but brief. In 1170 the Almohade prince occupied Seville, and the splendid mosque that still stands there is an enduring monument to his wealth and taste. Under the patronage of his successor flourished Averroës (1126–1198), the last and greatest of the medieval Muslim savants. This new pressure from Africa inspired new crusading zeal among the Spaniards. The Templars were encouraged to organize chapters in Spain, and in imitation of the crusaders, three similar military orders of Santiago, Calatrava, and Alcántara were formed to carry on the holy war in the peninsula. Muslim success reached its apogee shortly after Saladin's capture of Jerusalem, when in 1195 the Castilians, unsupported by the other Christian states, were routed by the Almohades at Alarcos. This disaster, following so soon after the failure of the Third Crusade in Syria, caused a crusade against the Almohades to be preached in the West. The Spanish princes, under pressure from Pope Innocent III, composed their quarrels and acted together. Crusaders from France crossed the Pyrenees to their assistance, and recruits came from the Italian cities. On the field of Las Navas de Tolosa in 1212 was fought the decisive battle, a Christian victory that marks the beginning of the end for Moorish rule in Spain. By the middle of the thirteenth century, Cordova and Seville were in Christian hands, and nothing remained to the Muslims but the little kingdom of Granada in the southeast, which maintained a precarious existence for another century and a half.

One result of the Third Crusade was a short-lived German interest in the situation in Palestine. This led in 1197 to the formation of another military order in imitation of the Hospitalers—the Teutonic Knights. But the real significance of this organization is to be found elsewhere than in Syria. Within less than

thirty years, the order transferred its efforts from fighting Muslims in the East to warring against pagans
in central Europe, first in Hungary, and then in Prussia.
From pope and emperor, the Knights' grand master,
Hermann von Salza, gained the grant in full sovereignty
—under papal suzerainty—of all lands conquered from
the heathen Prussians, an arrangement somewhat similar to the early idea of the Kingdom of Jerusalem.
Absorbing the existing order of the Knights of the
Sword of Livonia, the Teutonic Knights carried on for
a century a successful conquest of the southeastern
coastlands of the Baltic Sea. They established castles,
attracted German colonists, founded cities, and converted the natives to Christianity while reducing them
to serfdom. This ecclesiastical principality was a truly
civilizing force in a backward area. It maintained a
political existence long after occasion for crusading was
past. Eventually, in the sixteenth century, it became a
hereditary duchy and in the seventeenth century, by
an accident of inheritance, it became united to the
Margravate of Brandenberg to provide the basis for
the modern kingdom of Prussia.

Western Enemies of the Byzantine
Empire

Meanwhile, the attention of some of the Western Europeans was being somewhat distracted from the Latin
Kingdom in Syria to the Byzantine Empire. Alexius I
and his Comneni successors, helped by the victories of
the First Crusade, devoted themselves, during most of
the twelfth century to recovering lost territory and
reviving the prestige of the empire. Their reconquest
of Asia Minor was never complete, since the Seljuks
retained control of the interior. This unsatisfactor
result was due to the distracting difficulties the emperors had with their northern neighbors and focs,
the Bulgars and Serbs, and also to their persistent efforts to extend and maintain Byzantine suzerainty over

the crusading states in Syria. One of the chief hinder-
ances, however, to imperial ambition was the Venetian
trade monopoly. Under the original concession made
by Alexius in 1082 as a necessary part of his resistance
to Bohemund and his Normans, the Venetians had
come to enjoy in Constantinople privileges not unlike
the extraterritorial rights of Europeans in China in
more modern times. They had a strangle hold on the
empire's commerce. A large Venetian trading colony
occupied part of the imperial capital, an object of
envy to the Greek populace because of its wealth and
of patriotic and religious hostility because of its difference in nationality and creed. For the government,
these Venetians were an object of concern, not only
because they sapped the economic strength of the
empire, but because they were potential disturbers of
the peace by their quarrelsome relations with their
trade rivals from other Italian cities and their willingness to dabble in Byzantine politics by intriguing
with discontented and ambitious aristocrats in Constantinople. It was no doubt also apparent to an
impecunious emperor that the seizure of Venetian
property in the capital would be, temporarily, both
popular and profitable. Moreover, the Venetians were
constantly abusing their commercial privileges by indulging in piracy and slave-trading and bedeviling imperial foreign policy by warring on the Muslims at
sea irrespective of treaties and truces. Such advantages
as Alexius may have gained in 1082 were neutralized
in some degree by the fact that concessions accorded
the Venetians by the crusading states deflected to Syria
much of the trade that had formerly come to the
Bosporus. Also, the Venetians were finding it more
profitable to trade and ally with the Normans than
to fight against them.

The Normans, for their part, were just as hostile
toward the Byzantine Empire as in Robert Guiscard's
time, and considerably stronger. Bohemund, as prince
of Antioch, had been humiliated by Alexius and had

returned to western Europe to urge a crusade against the perfidious Greeks. Although this expedition, even with papal sanction, failed, it indicated clearly, even to contemporaries, the Norman willingness to use the crusade as a cloak for territorial ambitions at the expense of fellow Christians. With the founding of the Kingdom of Sicily in 1130 by Roger II, these ambitions became more grandiose, aiming at domination of the Mediterranean Sea. These new horizons led to efforts at conquest at the expense of the Muslims in North Africa. It also led the Norman kings to assume the role of protectors of the Christians in Syria and champions of the Latins in Constantinople. They were cousins to the princes of Antioch, and it was prompt assistance from Sicily that saved Tyre from Saladin. The agitation in the West for a combined effort to conquer Byzantium, started by Bohemund, became an important part of Norman policy. The Latins of the West became more and more receptive to this idea. Despite efforts of the responsible leaders on both sides, the armies of the Second and Third crusades engaged at times in pillaging when traversing Byzantine territory, and even captured Byzantine towns in their march eastward. For the Byzantine Caesars, the German emperors on these expeditions could be regarded as upstart rivals. All this made for suspicion, friction, and hard feeling. There were some crusaders who thought that a Latin conquest of Constantinople would heal a political as well as a religious schism. Such an achievement could be rationalized as a useful, desirable preliminary, even a necessity, for recovering and holding the Holy Places.

A Byzantine revival under the later Comneni led to renewed and intensified conflict with the Western states. The emperors attempted to abolish the Venetian monopoly, to oust the Venetian colony, to counterbalance Venetian privileges by grants to the Genoese and Pisans, their rivals, and to overawe the Adriatic republic by conquering Dalmatia. The Venetians replied by making an alliance with the Norman kingdom, raiding in the Aegean, and preparing a naval attack against Constantinople. Indeed, in 1155 a Norman fleet actually forced the Dardanelles, but without decisive results. In 1172 the emperor felt strong enough to seize the Venetian quarter in the imperial city, and a general war threatened, with the Western enemies of Venice and the Normans allied to the Byzantines. When peace was made, however, the emperor agreed to pay the republic an indemnity for its losses. Most of this was never paid. The Comnenian revival was just strong enough to alarm the Venetians and to excite them to desperate measures, without being strong enough to break their grip on the empire.

In the political confusion at Constantinople, which marked the decline and extinction of the Comneni in 1185, the Western enemies of Byzantium saw their opportunity. One of the preliminary phases of that confusion was marked by a massacre of the hated Latins by a mob from Constantinople urged on by the Greek clergy. The Norman king, as avenger of his coreligionists, invaded the empire, claiming to act in support of a pretender to the throne. He advanced well into Macedonia toward Constantinople before his forces were beaten. The Venetians became convinced that conquest of the Byzantine Empire was necessary as a means of guaranteeing the personal safety of their citizens as well as desirable for commercial advantages. In the crisis produced by Saladin's victories, followed by the Third Crusade, attention became centered upon the Syrian coast where, as we have noted, the English king conquered the Byzantine island of Cyprus and set up Guy of Lusignan as king there.

The Fourth Crusade

The succession to the Norman throne, first of a woman and then of a child, paralyzed the Sicilian kingdom. This temporarily relieved pressure from the West

against the Byzantines. When news of the failure of
the Third Crusade reached France, certain of the
greater nobles vowed to go to the rescue of the Latin
Kingdom. Pope Innocent III gave his support and sent
itinerant preachers to stir up the faithful. None of
the Western kings responded, and popular enthusiasm
was not as great as a century before. As encouragement,
the pope granted limited indulgences for all those who
listened to the preachers, whether or not they took
crusading vows. Recruiting was more orderly and less
haphazard than before, and a sort of baronial leadership was set up which promised to be more effective.
Experience of previous expeditions showed that movement eastward by sea was to be preferred to the long
marches overland. This became even more important
considering that King Richard had indicated that
Egypt, being now the center of Muslim power, should
be recognized as the objective of crusader attack.

Since an attack upon Egypt must necessarily be
made by sea, the crusading chiefs turned to Venice,
the leading naval power, for transport and contracted
to pay for the use of the Venetian fleet. In such a
situation, the Venetian Republic enjoyed the advantage
of a seller's market, which Venetian leaders were prepared to exploit. When the crusading bands assembled
at Venice, their numbers were much below the expectations and promises of their leaders. The latter, in consequence lacking sufficient funds, could not fulfil their
contract with the republic. Having profitable trade arrangements with the sultan of Egypt, the Venetians
were cool to the idea of an attack in that direction,
but they did not reveal this to the crusaders. After
considerable haggling, in which the crusaders, being
marooned on one of the Venetian islands, were at a
great disadvantage, it was agreed that they could meet
their obligations by joining in the capture of the
Dalmatian city of Zara, a trade rival described by the
Venetians as a nest of pirates. Pope Innocent sternly
forbade the pilgrims turning their arms against Chris-

tians, but the crusading chiefs felt that they had no alternative. Zara was easily captured, and the crusader debts to the Venetians paid from the spoil. The pope excommunicated the whole expedition. Later he raised the ban for all except the Venetians who remained indifferent. Such flagrant defiance of a most powerful pope shows how little control over crusading existed.

The expedition might then have proceeded to Egypt, but for the appearance at Zara of a Byzantine princeling. Alexius Angelus was a refugee from Constantinople, the victim of a palace revolution. He came asking for help toward his restoration to the throne, making large promises of money and aid to be forthcoming after that happy event. For the Venetians with trade interests in Egypt, such a deflection of the expedition was not unwelcome, while the opportunity for intervening at Constantinople seemed too good to be lost. The pope forbade such action. Those crusaders of the rank and file, who took crusading seriously, protested. But the leaders, arguing that the holy war could be carried on more effectively by way of the Byzantine capital with the aid of an imperial Greek ally, were persuaded, and the expedition sailed for the Straits. With this military and naval support Alexius was restored to the imperial throne in the summer of 1203. He then found himself unable to fulfill the extravagant promises made to his crusader allies, partly because of the Greek popular hatred for the Latins. The crusaders waited impatiently, and wintered outside the capital. In February a popular insurrection deposed and killed Alexius. The Westerners proceeded to besiege the city. It was during this period of mob violence that Phidias' statue of Athena—which Constantine had carried away from the Parthenon—was destroyed. The crusader siege culminated on April 11, 1204, in an assault in which the richest and most civilized city in Europe was stormed, sacked, and burned by a host of armed pilgrims vowed to recover the Holy Sepulcher. Religious ardor showed itself in the eagerness with which the looters plundered the Greek churches of the holy relics accumulated over the centuries. It was at this time that the Venetians carried off the four bronze horses, which still adorn the façade of St. Mark's Cathedral.

Instead of being scandalized at this misuse of a crusade, the West exulted at the destruction of the hated schismatics. Even the pope, whose orders had been repeatedly flouted, contented himself with expectation of healing the schism by reunion of the Greek and Latin churches under papal authority, an important objective of papal crusading policy from the beginning. The crusaders, for their part, proceeded to elect one of their leaders emperor, to divide the Byzantine parts of the Balkan peninsula into fiefs distributed among themselves, and to assign Aegean islands and commercial privileges to the Venetians. A Latin Empire was thus created like the Latin Kingdom of Jerusalem, but more brazenly an adventurer state brought into existence through the fears and ambitions of Venice and the unscrupulous statesmanship of the Doge Dondolo. Refugee Greek governments were set up and maintained in Asia Minor at Nicaea and Trebizond. In little less than sixty years, a Greek restoration at Constantinople was effected. The schism remained unhealed, and the triumphant crusaders did nothing further about recovering the Holy Sepulcher.

The Fifth Crusade

Despite the deflection of the Fourth Crusade, which may well have appeared to contemporaries as something temporary, preaching of a crusade continued in the West. One peculiar feature of this effort was an expression of religious revivalism reminiscent of 1095, which is called the Children's Crusade. In 1212 two youthful preachers—one in France, the other in Germany—led columns of young people to the sea expecting God miraculously to part the waters so that

they could march to Jerusalem. Since this miracle did
not take place, most of those who had survived the long
march returned home. A few who took ship were either
lost at sea or captured by Muslim corsairs and sold
into slavery. Pope Innocent still hoped to arouse Western Christendom to effective military action, although
the Latins in the fragmentary crusader states along
the coast of Syria were not eager for another Western
army. They had come to terms with Saladin's successor,
living in peace with their Muslim neighbors to the
scandal of fanatical pilgrims from the West.

Papal efforts succeeded in organizing a Fifth Crusade.
Under the ardent leadership of a papal legate, it made
a victorious attack in 1218 upon Damietta on the
eastern edge of the Nile delta. The sultan of Egypt,
seriously threatened by certain Muslim rivals in Syria,
offered to surrender Jerusalem and return the True
Cross captured by Saladin as the price of regaining
Damietta. Hopeful of continued and greater successes
in Egypt, and asserting that no terms should be made
with infidels, the legate refused. It was at this time
that Francis of Assissi came to Egypt to make a personal appeal for peace and to attempt the conversion
of the Muslims by preaching. The sultan received him
kindly and listened to him, but nothing came of it.
When in 1221 the Christian army advanced on Cairo,
it met with an overwhelming defeat, which put it at
the sultan's mercy. The legate was forced to ask for
terms. He saved the army by surrendering Damietta.
The sultan promised to return the True Cross, but
it had disappeared and was never recovered.

The Mongols

The overthrow of the Byzantine Empire by the Fourth
Crusade reopened Asia Minor to the Turks, but the
interest of the Muslims in resisting the crusaders or
expelling them from Syria was distracted in the thirteenth century by the appearance in Persia and west-

ern Asia of conquering Mongol hordes. In 1206 a
Mongolian chieftain, having subjugated his neighbors,
assumed the title Genghis Khan ("Mighty Ruler") and
proceeded to conquer China and Central Asia. He organized his followers into a highly disciplined, mounted
army, which could move rapidly, live off the country,
endure extreme hardship, and fight with skill and
desperate boldness. Its chief was an extraordinary
genius who inspired blind confidence. In attacking
prosperous countries he permitted unrestrained pillage
to his followers and practiced extremes of ruthless
cruelty upon his opponents. In consequence, the Mongol
horde became irresistible, both by its skill and by the
terror that it inspired. The regions that it conquered
suffered destruction and depopulation unprecedented
since the days of the Assyrians. Although the Mongols
were heathen, the caliph of Bagdad was willing to use
them against his Persian enemies, and Genghis Khan's
invasion of western Asia in 1219 somewhat paralleled
the Seljuk intervention in the eleventh century. Although this first Mongol invasion was confined to eastern Persia, it contributed to the anarchy prevailing in
the Middle East and opened the way for later attacks.
In 1231 hordes ravaged Mesopotamia, stirring the
Egyptians and the western Turks to combine for
protection. It may have been a desire to conciliate
the Christians in apprehension of Mongol attack that
led the sultan of Egypt in 1229 to surrender Jerusalem
to Emperor Frederick II, who was then crusading to
the Holy Land and was quite content to gain the
city by diplomacy, even with infidels, instead of by
fighting. (He was excommunicate at the time, even
though a crusader, and his diplomatic success was de-
nounced by the pope.) This Christian recovery of the
Holy City, however, was short-lived, because within
fifteen years the Mongols overran Syria, devastated the
country, and sacked Jerusalem. But at that time Christian interest in the Levant was small, because the
Mongols were invading Europe also. Having occupied

Russia, they invaded Hungary in 1241, burned its capital, and rode to the very shores of the Adriatic. Fortunately for Europe the necessity of electing a new khan caused them to withdraw over the Carpathians while their leaders returned to Mongolia.

The most formidable Mongol onslaught came in the middle of the century when Hulagu, the grandson of Genghis Khan, set out to conquer all western Asia. Even the mountain fastnesses of the Assassins fell before him. In February 1258 his forces stormed Bagdad, capturing the caliph. Certain Muslims warned him that if the blood of the caliph were spilled, the world would be darkened and an earthquake would engulf the Mongols, so Hulagu put the caliph and his son in sacks and set his horsemen to trample them to death. So ended the Abbassid Caliphate of Bagdad. As an enemy of Islam, Hulagu favored Jews and Christians. The papacy and the Latin princes of Syria looked to him as a possible ally against a common foe. It was hoped that through this connection the Holy Land might be recovered without military effort from Europe. It was hoped that the Mongols would become Christians and that through them the Muslims would be totally destroyed. Hulagu's capture of Mosul and Aleppo seemed to promise some such result. Damascus submitted—only Egypt remained to fight for Islam.

The Mamelukes

The latter state was fortunate at that moment, for power had been seized by a vigorous military oligarchy, the Mamelukes. Originally, as their name indicates, these had been members of the slave bodyguard organized by Saladin's successors. By buying sturdy young Turks, Kurds, Circassians, and Georgians, educating them in arms, organizing them in troops, conferring upon them fiefs and pensions, and appointing their leaders to high political positions, the Egyptian sultans created an organized military aristocracy, with a notable *esprit de corps,* and real fighting power. They demonstrated the latter effectively in 1217 against the Fifth Crusade, which had captured Damietta, and again in 1248 at El Mansûra when they annihilated a Christian army and captured its leader, King Louis IX of France. Like the Turkish guard at Bagdad in former times, the Mamelukes discovered that they could make and unmake sultans with ease, that, indeed, the most vigorous and ambitious of their own leaders could aspire to the throne. One of the most capable of these, Beibars, distinguished himself by winning a decisive victory over the Mongols near Nazareth in 1260. On the strength of this achievement he assassinated his lord and became sultan in his place. It is reasonable to suppose that this Egyptian victory saved from destruction the flourishing Muslim civilization centered in Cairo—and reflected in the *Arabian Nights.* Ambitious to imitate Saladin although lacking his personal qualities, Beibars resumed the holy war against the crusader states. The Christians in Syria, regarding the Mongols as friends, urged Hulagu to renew his invasion of Syria in the spring of 1264, when the Muslim soldiers would be at home and their horses out to pasture; but the Mongol khan died the next year without responding to this appeal. The Mamelukes, however, now recognized the Christians as dangerous enemies ready to aid the formidable Mongol invader, so they turned while there was yet time to complete the conquests of Saladin. In 1268 the Egyptians captured Antioch. A new crusade organized in 1270 by Louis IX to succor the Latin East turned aside at the urging of the ruler of the Norman kingdom in southern Italy to capture Tunis in North Africa. Here the French king died, and the crusading army accomplished nothing. In 1289 Tripoli fell to the Egyptians, and finally in 1291 they took Acre by storm. All the other Christian towns quickly surrendered. Latin rule in Syria came to an end. In Cyprus a king of Jerusalem continued to rule.

Western Disillusionment

Europe regarded these events with indifference. Two
centuries of crusading had been disillusioning. Difficulties and obstacles to success, of which the first
crusaders had been ignorant, were now matters of
general knowledge. The futility of relying upon armies
of temporary pilgrims had become obvious. Papal leadership had become an object of criticism and attack
that sometimes took the form of anticrusading propaganda. This was particularly the case when various
popes launched so-called crusades against enemies of
the Church or of the papacy. It seemed that the pious
motives of the First Crusade were giving way to the
worldly ambitions of popes, princes, and maritime
republics, although the faithful were still being ex-
horted to take crusading vows in the same terms as
before. Under the guise of healing the schism, a
crusade had been used to overthrow and conquer, not
the Holy Land in infidel hands, but the principal
Christian state in the East. From the blow struck by
the Fourth Crusade, the Greek (Byzantine) Empire, although it regained Constantinople in 1261, never recovered. When, in the fourteenth century, the Ottoman Turks invaded Europe, the Greeks, who had been
in times past a bulwark against Saracens and Seljuks,
could offer no effectual resistance. Even the Syrian principalities, remnants of the Kingdom of Jerusalem, were
weakened by the establishment of the Latin Empire.
Many of the adventurers who might otherwise have
reinforced the Latin Kingdom went off to seek their
fortunes in the more promising regions of Greece.
Crusading ardor was further diverted when the papacy
preached holy wars of a new sort. The Albigensian
Crusade of 1208 in southern France promised all the
spiritual advantages, with even more generous indulgences than were gained by the hazardous journey
to the Holy Land. With no Turkish warriors as opponents, the chances of success were more promising.

Warriors flocked to southern France to kill heretics and conquer territory instead of going to help the sorely pressed Kingdom of Jerusalem. This crusade was conducted with a devastating brutality comparable to that of the Mongols. Later in the century the papacy's political struggle with Emperor Frederick II and his heirs in Italy became so bitter that crusade was preached against them. The fact that Frederick, by marrying the heiress to the Latin Kingdom, claimed to be king of Jerusalem, that in 1228 he went crusading to the Holy Land and regained Jerusalem by negotiation the following year, did not save him from excommunication by the pope, nor from having Jerusalem laid under an interdict. Papal hostility was so bitter that the pious were urged to enlist under the banner of the Church to fight their fellow Christians in Italy for the advancement of papal political interests. Ghibelline propaganda made much of this to discredit the papacy and, incidentally, to discredit crusading also. Indeed, it appeared that any enemy of the papacy, either the king of Aragon, or the Roman nobles, or the barons of England, could be classified with the Muslims as fit objects for a holy war. Crusading had become a mere recruiting device.

Diversion of Crusading Energies

Nothing illustrates more strikingly the diversion of the crusading spirit from its original purpose in the Holy Land than the later history of the Teutonic Knights, already mentioned, and of the Templars. The former, it is true, maintained headquarters at Acre until the city's fall, but their chief attention had long been turned toward the prospect of conquering new lands in eastern Europe, one more alluring and rewarding than anything in Syria. Adventurers, pious and otherwise, like Chaucer's knight or Henry Bolingbroke, later King Henry IV of England, turned to this new field of activity. As Christianity replaced

paganism in this area, the occasion for spreading the
One True Faith disappeared. In the course of the
thirteenth and fourteenth centuries, the Knights, absorbed in conquering, defending, and ruling their
border provinces, lost all connection with the East,
forgot their original religious zeal, and became a landed
aristocracy, warring against neighboring Russians and
Poles without religious pretenses. The Templars remained active in the holy war until the Muslim conquest of Syria was complete, so active, in fact, that
in the disastrous battles that marked Saladin's reconquest, the membership in the order resident in the
East was almost annihilated. But the important activities of the order in its later years had come to be
financial rather than military. The Templars had
become wealthy from extensive grants made to them
in Europe by pious persons desiring to support the
cause for which the order was presumably organized.
Their strongholds, "temples," in the West were safe
places for kings and popes to deposit their treasure.
Their international character gave them opportunities
to play the role of bankers in Europe and the Levant,
and to this useful function they devoted much of
their energy. To Western rulers the order looked like
a secret society no longer performing the function for
which it had been created. Its wealth and power,
together with the privileges conferred on the order
by various popes, tended to make it a sort of state
within a state, arousing the hostility of the secular
clergy and the jealousy of the king of France. Their
wealth excited the cupidity of the latter, Philip IV,
grandson of St. Louis, last of the genuine crusaders,
with the result that in 1312 he trumped up charges
of heresy against the Knights, extracted confessions
under torture from some of them, pressured the pope
into suppressing the order, burned Jacques de Molay,
the last grand master, at the stake, and appropriated
a large share of the order's property.

Only the Hospitalers, benefiting from the destruction

St. Louis, a prisoner in Egypt during the Sixth Crusade, 1248–
1252. Engraving. *(New York Public Library)*

of the Templars, continued, after the fall of Acre, to cooperate with the Latin principalities in the East. With Cyprus as a base, and in alliance with the Genoese, they conquered Rhodes from the Byzantines and maintained themselves there until the sixteenth century, serving as a center for trade and as a Latin outpost against the Ottoman Turks. These island states of Rhodes and Cyprus also received support from the Venetians, who, after the Fourth Crusade, occupied part of the Peloponnesus and the Aegean archipelago and sought to monopolize the Black Sea trade. Even after the Greek restoration at Constantinople in 1261, the Venetians maintained some hold on the islands. But in 1669 the Turkish sultan drove them from Crete, their last possession in the eastern Mediterranean. The Hospitalers in Rhodes carried on a guerrilla warfare at sea against the Muslims, a sort of remnant of crusading. In this way they became enough of a piratical nuisance that Sultan Suleiman the Magnificent in 1522 made the military and naval effort necessary, in the face of a heroic defense, to capture the island fortress. He permitted the Knights to withdraw to Malta, from which base they carried on intermittent aristocratic piracy against the North African Muslims until 1798. In that year General Bonaparte, en route to Egypt with a French army, occupied the island and ended their rule. Thus the upstart child of the French Revolution obliterated the last political vestiges of the crusades. The organization still exists as a noble order of chivalry, the Knights of Malta, in an unchivalric age, a shadowy remnant of a remote heroic past.

But as early as the twelfth and thirteenth centuries, crusading had excited hostility and doubt. Secular authorities, from an early date, disliked the extension of ecclesiastical jurisdiction under the cloak of protecting absent crusaders. Royal counselors, concerned for home affairs, sometimes deplored the dissipation of power and resources to the not always observable good results of crusading. The Sieur de Joinville, St.

Louis' biographer, resisted the king's urgings to take
the cross. He remarks:

I thought that all who advised him to go on the crusade
committed a mortal sin because France was then at peace
within and at peace with all her neighbors. And after he
left the kingdom got steadily worse. — They committed a
great sin, those who advised him to take the cross when
his body was as weak as it was. — Yet ill as he was, if he
had remained in France, he could have lived longer and
have done a great deal of good.

St. Louis was a most unfortunate crusader. On his
first expedition in 1249–1250, he, with his whole army,
was taken prisoner by the Egyptians and held for ransom. On the second, against Tunis in 1270, the crusading force accomplished nothing, lost heavily from
sickness, and the king was among the dead. Serious
doubts arose that crusading was pleasing to God when
failure and misfortune could happen to such saints as
Bernard and Louis. Said Friar Salimbene, "nor does it
seem like the Divine Will that the Holy Sepulcher
should be recovered since the great number attempting
it have labored in vain." Perhaps God willed it in
1095, but not in the years following. Sometimes crusades appeared as devices for levying taxes. This excited complaint from both clergy and laity, although
kings showed complacency when the papacy permitted
the proceeds of such levies to be turned to royal uses
in return for concessions. The practice of permitting
those reluctant to fulfill crusading vows to redeem themselves by paying money, encouraged anticlerical critics
to charge that priests were exploiting crusading for
revenue.

Cyprus as a Crusading State

Nevertheless, the idea of crusading persisted and propaganda in its support continued long after the fall of

Acre. Widespread popular preaching, however, was notably absent or ineffective from the thirteenth century on. The continued existence in the Levant of a Latin crusading state in Cyprus gave some political basis for urging further crusading efforts. Here the Lusignans were kings and, eventually, through the vagaries of intermarriage and resulting hereditary claims, added the title King of Jerusalem to that of King of Cyprus. As the remnants of the Latin Kingdom in Syria were conquered by the Egyptians, the crusader nobility there found a safe refuge in Cyprus, where they received new fiefs. Content with these, their eagerness to attempt reconquests on the mainland was limited. In Cyprus was drawn up that body of customary law known as the Assizes of Jerusalem. This code illustrates the character of a truly feudal state formed *de novo* by the baronage. The safeguarding of the rights of feudal nobles is fundamental. It might seem that a state as dangerously exposed to hostile encirclement as was the Kingdom of Jerusalem needed more powerful, authoritarian leadership than a feudal nobility, jealous of its rights, was willing to accept. If so, this was a weakness that the crusaders' states never overcame, and one that contributed to their ultimate destruction. There is a touch of historic irony in the fact that, in the kingdom of Cyprus, these feudal principles were being maintained and put into definite recorded form at a time when they were being significantly modified in the West through the development of royal power tending toward national monarchies. Whatever the relationship to the legal-political customs of the original Latin Kingdom to be found in the assizes, in the written form that survives, they belong to the kingdom of Cyprus.

For the kings of Cyprus and the refugee nobles from Syria, recovery of the Holy Land seemed, in the circumstances, a project of doubtful feasibility. Until 1291 they clung to the Syrian coast, but tried to avoid dissipating Cypriote resources in a hopeless defense of the mainland. With the loss of the Syrian ports, those of Cyprus became important, flourishing emporia for Levantine trade. Raiding Muslim shores could be a profitable form of continuing the holy war, but the cause of the Holy Sepulcher loomed small in such activities. King Peter I (1359–1369), believing that he had a divine mission to recover the Holy Places, attempted to renew serious crusading. To do this he founded a new military order, the Order of the Sword, and aimed to gain a base on the mainland from which to launch a campaign of reconquest. Opportunity offered in 1361 to capture Adalia on the southern coast of Asia Minor and Peter exploited it successfully. (The Christians held this place until 1373.) In order to follow up his victory King Peter toured Europe in 1362–1363 to stir up the Western rulers to a new crusade and himself to enlist recruits. Everywhere he was welcomed, feted, and encouraged with promises more or less vague. Rulers like King John of France took crusading vows but failed, for one reason or another, to fulfill them. Peter did enlist fighting men, and he gained the naval support of Venice and Genoa. The pope at Avignon tried to persuade the companies —those mercenary fighting men thrown out of work by a peaceful interval in the Hundred Years' War— who were maintaining themselves by ravaging France to enlist under the cross and so win forgiveness for their multiple and enormous sins. These men-at-arms, however, preferred to risk damnation and to seek their fortunes in the political struggles going on among Christians in Italy and Spain. Peter's rendezvous was fixed at Rhodes, but the ultimate object of attack was deliberately kept secret from the Italian naval powers. That object was Alexandria. In October 1365 the expedition appeared unexpectedly before that Egyptian port, took it by assault, and subjected it to sack for three days. Having collected masses of plunder, most of the crusading army, rather than defend their conquest, insisted on withdrawing to Cyprus and from there going home. The Venetians reported falsely in the West that King Peter had made peace with the sultan. This forestalled possible reinforcements. Indeed the count of Savoy was already heading an expedition to assist Peter, but this false news encouraged him to consider rescuing the Greek emperor, a relative, from captivity among the Bulgarians. He satisfied his crusading zeal by killing Turks on the Gallipoli Peninsula.

As a measure of the new status of crusading, this episode is enlightening. The impulse and ardor came from a Levantine ruler and seems to have evoked little comparable response, although much verbal approval. Many of the recruits were mercenaries who had to be paid. They were looking for plunder and quit when they got it. This made their success ephemeral as far as crusading went. Their destruction of Alexandria, another great cultural center, may be placed beside the comparable sack of Constantinople in the previous century. For the sultans of Egypt, the lesson was clear. Cyprus was a menace to be curbed and if possible subdued in self-defense. Opportunity was delayed until 1426. In that year the Mameluke sultan invaded the island, defeated the Cypriote army, carried the Christian king captive to Cairo, and imposed Egyptian suzerainty with a levy of tribute upon this last crusader state. When in 1474 the last Lusignan king, an infant, died, his mother, Catherine Cornaro, a Venetian noblewoman, after reigning herself for fifteen years, abdicated in favor of the Venetian Republic, which continued to pay tribute to the Egyptian sultan. By this date the Muslim threat came from the Ottoman Turks at Constantinople. In 1571 the Turks conquered Cyprus after a heroic defense and wiped out the last vestiges of the crusades in the Levant.

Crusades to Smyrna and Mahdia

If we turn back to consider the agitation for crusading in the West after the fall of Acre, we are struck with

the amount of literary propaganda urging new crusades
and discussing what should be done to ensure success.
It does not sound like Peter the Hermit, and it clearly
did not arouse popular enthusiasm of the eleventh-
century sort, but the sincerity of the writers should not
be questioned, even when they state that general European peace and reforms of the Church in head and
members were necessary preliminaries. Such prerequi-
sites would indeed postpone crusading until the Greek
Kalends. It was realistic, perhaps, to address these
appeals to kings and princes rather than to the peoples.
Popes persistently advocated crusading and urged peace
upon Western rulers, but none of them aroused their
hearers as Urban II had in 1095. Two centuries of
effort had been disillusioning. But several Western
rulers made elaborate plans. King Philip VI of France
was halted in the midst of preparing an expedition
by the outbreak of the Hundred Years' War. King John,
his son, took the cross but died before he could do
anything. In 1344 a league of the Hospitalers, the
king of Cyprus, and the republics of Genoa and Venice,
sponsored by the pope, organized a fleet that captured
Smyrna. Its primary purpose was the suppression of
the piracy for which this port provided a base. The
acclaim excited by this Christian victory stimulated
Humbert II, Dauphin of Viennois, to volunteer to lead
a crusading army to exploit this success. Such an expedition did reach Asia Minor but those and later
efforts to push inland failed, and the dauphin accomplished little. Losing heart he came home, abdicated
(willing his state to the French king's heir), and became a Dominican monk. The Hospitalers held Smyrna
until 1402 when Tamerlane's Mongols stormed the city,
massacred the inhabitants, and razed the walls. When
the Mongol tide receded, the Ottoman Turks took
over.

The western Mediterranean during the later Middle
Ages continued to be an area of sporadic conflict between Christian and Muslim. King James of Aragon

launched a crusade against the Balearic Islands in
1229. Within six years they were completely subdued,
and James enjoyed the sobriquet of "the Conqueror"
in consequence. Modern historians see in this the first
step in the creation of Spain's overseas empire. By the
end of the century Aragonese rule had been extended
to Sicily, but this was at the expense of the Norman
kingdom. That realm in Italy had been taken over
by Charles of Anjou, a younger brother of Louis IX
of France, but no saint. He continued the aggressive
policies of his predecessors toward the Byzantines and
the Muslims of North Africa. This accounts for the
direction of King Louis' crusade in 1270 to Tunis,
which proved to be a calamitous failure. The only
danger now from the African Muslims arose from their
piratical activities, which menaced Mediterranean commerce. A century later the Genoese found these sufficiently troublesome to warrant a punitive expedition
against the corsairs. Genoa was a strong naval power
rivaling Venice. Through close relations with the restored Greek emperors at Constantinople, the Genoese
had extended their trade into the Black Sea where
they had a colony at Kaffa in the Crimea. For a time
they also imposed their domination upon the kings of
Cyprus. A mere punitive expedition against North
African pirates would have only limited European
appeal. But the idea of a holy war against the infidel appealed to the king of France and attracted the
support of the French chivalry eager for adventure.
The king's uncle, the Duke of Bourbon, favored
a crusade and begged to be allowed to lead one. An
expedition of considerable size under his command
sailed to attack Mahdia, the Tunisian capital, in 1390.
A siege of nine weeks produced a stalemate. The crusaders could not take the city, nor could the Muslims
raise the siege. The Genoese then negotiated a peace
treaty favorable for trade, which the crusading duke
reluctantly accepted. On the way home, the Genoese
persuaded the crusaders to attack Sardinia, said to be

occupied by pirates from Aragon, and to install Genoese
garrisons there, but failed to get comparable action
against Pisa. As a holy war, this crusade did little; but
as an effort to improve Genoese trade, it was reasonably successful. The duke of Bourbon was acclaimed
as a returning hero, and King Charles VI took the
cross, vowing to crush the Muslim power. Nothing came
of it.

The Crusade of Nicopolis

Elsewhere crusading ardor flared, and directed its attention eastward. Since the middle of the thirteenth
century, the Ottoman Turks had become increasingly
menacing in Asia Minor and the Balkan Peninsula.
An unusual succession of vigorous sultans and an organized, disciplined army imbued with a religious fighting spirit made the Ottomans a more formidable power
than any Christian Europe had previously encountered.
This, too, at a time when the restored Greek Empire
was much too weak to imitate its Byzantine predecessor
as guardian of the gate to Europe. Indeed, the Ottomans gained their first foothold on Gallipoli as allies
to a contender for the Greek throne. During the second
half of the fourteenth century, the Turkish sultans
were engaged in subduing Asia Minor and the Balkan
areas held by Bulgars and Serbs. The walls of Constantinople still held them at bay. In June 1389 the
Serbs suffered an overwhelming defeat at Kossovo.
This brought the Turkish-Muslim frontier to the
Danube, a menace to the kingdom of Hungary. King
Sigismund appealed to the West.

To this Hungarian appeal French chivalry responded
with enthusiasm. Pope Boniface IX proclaimed a crusade. The aging duke of Burgundy, Philip the Bold,
gave his support and sent his son and heir, John the
Fearless, to lead an expedition which many of the chief
nobles of France joined. Fighting men from Germany,
England, Spain, and elsewhere responded to the call.

Froissart estimated the Christian forces at a hundred thousand men. This is difficult to accept, although the absence of a problem of sea transport makes it more nearly possible. The Western leaders, more disposed than the Hungarian king to despise the barbarous Turks, of whose fighting qualities they were completely ignorant, asserted boastfully that they could "conquer all Turkey, and even advance to the kingdom of Persia." A victory over the Turks, they said, would enable them to "conquer Syria and the Holy Land, and deliver Jerusalem out of the hands of the Sultan and the enemies of God." This goal they were impatient to reach. Their insistence overcame Sigismund's reluctance, and the crusading army crossed the Danube. Sultan Bajazet promptly abandoned the siege of Constantinople and moved north. On September 26, 1396, a pitched battle was fought at Nicopolis. The Turks won an overwhelming victory. The Christian army was destroyed. Large numbers of prisoners, including most of the Western leaders, were captured. The most important were held for ransom; the others were massacred. Enthusiasm for further crusading could hardly endure such a disaster. Bajazet resumed the siege of Constantinople.

Failure to Save Constantinople

The imperial city was saved at this time by Tamerlane, a new Mongol conqueror from the east. At Angora in 1402 he defeated and captured the Ottoman sultan. This provided the Christians in southeastern Europe with a breathing spell for a generation. Sultan Murad II (1421–1451) resumed the conquest of the Balkans. The Greek position was desperate. The emperor came in person to the Council of Ferrara, accompanied by his brother, the patriarch of Constantinople, seeking Western help against the Turk. Pope Eugenius IV, eager to discredit the antipapal Council of Basel, thought he saw himself in a position to reunite the two

Churches, an object of papal policy for nearly four
centuries. This would be the preliminary to a great
European crusade to save Constantinople. In 1439
Greek desperation forced the emperor to accept papal
terms and agree to make the Eastern Church subject
to the pope. In the East, the people and clergy repudiated this forced union. If they must choose they preferred Muslim rule, which was contemptuously tolerant
of Christian sectarianism, to submission to the hated
Latins. Pope Eugenius did proclaim a crusade and
sent a cardinal-legate into Hungary to advance the
cause. King Ladislas of Hungary and his chief lieutenant, John Hunyadi, had carried on successful campaigns
against the Turk, which had forced Sultan Murad in
1443 to offer a truce on favorable terms for ten years.
Both parties swore solemn oaths to observe this agreement. But the pope and his legate urged immediate
renewal of what they expected to be a victorious campaign. The cardinal absolved the Hungarian king from
his oath, since it had been made to an infidel and was
not, in consequence, morally binding. Ladislas led an
invading army across the Danube only to be severely
defeated at Varna in November 1444. Both the king
and the cardinal-legate were killed. There was no
further interference with Turkish efforts to take Constantinople, which was besieged and captured nine
years later. The great church of St. Sofia, Orthodox
Christianity's chief shrine, was transformed into a
mosque, a monument to the triumph of Islam.

Last Papal Efforts at Crusading

The election in 1455 of Calixitus III brought to the
papacy a pope ardent for a holy war against the
Turks, one who sought to arouse the European princes
and to collect funds. Only in Hungary was there any
response. Here the dangers of Ottoman power and ag-
gressiveness were patent. Friar John of Capistrano
zealously forwarded the crusading cause and found in

John Hunyadi a still-vigorous leader aware of the necessities of national defense. Under his command, a Christian army won a signal victory in July 1456 which forced the sultan to raise the siege of Belgrade. Christian Europe cheered this triumph, but took no action to follow it up. A month later both Hunyadi and Friar John died of the plague. However, the Turkish advance was checked at the Danube for nearly three quarters of a century.

Pius II, who succeeded Calixtus as pope, was no less disposed to urge the necessity for a crusade. Realizing that only a common European effort could hope to achieve results he invited the western princes to attend an international congress at Mantua. Here, under papal auspices, the necessary plans could be made. Presumably, Pius envisaged a more grandiose Council of Clermont. Here was a formal effort by the Roman pontiff to put himself at the head of a united Christendom to wage holy war against a dangerous Muslim aggressor. The sentimental appeal of regaining the Holy Sepulcher, which was potent in 1095, may have lost much of its power through the repeated failures, but it should have been replaced by a realistic appreciation of the actual menace of Turkish power already established in Europe. Pius was statesman enough to see this. On June 1, 1459, the pope in person at Mantua was prepared to open his congress, but no European prince had appeared or sent representatives. During the summer, envoys from some lesser princes arrived, more ready to negotiate on ecclesiastical matters of local interest to their masters than to discuss crusading. In late September, the pope formally opened the congress with a speech notable for its humanistic eloquence. He urged his hearers to "fight bravely for the law of God" and invoked memories of 1095.

Would that there were here to-day Godfrey or Baldwin, Eustace, Hugh the Great, Boemund [Bohemund], Tancred,

and the rest who in days gone by won back Jerusalem!
They would not have suffered us to speak so long, but
rising from their seats, as once they did before our predecessor Urban II, they would have cried with one voice,
"God wills it, God wills it!"

No imitators of past heroes were present and this
Renaissance audience sat silent, however much it may
have appreciated the pope's oratory. To prove his sincerity, which many of his contemporaries much doubted,
Pius declared his intention, despite his uncertain health,
to go himself on the expedition. The congress declared
war on the Turk. General plans were discussed and the
envoys returned home. The pope wrote a letter to the
sultan exhorting him to become a Christian. It received no reply. In October 1463 a crusade was of-
ficially proclaimed by papal bull. Friars preached
zealously in different countries, and crusaders began
to gather at various Italian ports only to find no available transport. The pope himself, having formally
taken the cross in St. Peter's in June 1464, proceeded
to Ancona to join the expedition, but the disappointed
crusaders there were already beginning to disperse to
their homes. Within a month of his arrival at Ancona,
the pope died, and the crusade died with him. What
may be said to have started gloriously in 1095 at Clermont fizzled at Ancona in 1464. Pius II, it would seem,
is more entitled than St. Louis to be called the "Last
Crusader."

Iberian Reconquest Completed
and Extended

In the Iberian Peninsula, however, Christian successes
against the Muslims had continued. In Portugal as in
Spain, the reconquest had been carried on with the
help of a local crusading order, organized in 1162,
the Order of St. Benedict of Aviz, so named from its
headquarters on the Moorish frontier. When the king

of France forced the pope to suppress the Order of the Temple in 1312, the Portuguese king took the Templars in Portugal under his protection. In 1318 he absorbed these knights into a newly created Order of Christ. (This order continues today as an important papal organization.) Early in the fifteenth century Prince Henry, a younger son of King John of Portugal, became grand master of the Order of Christ. Since there were no more Moors in Portugal, and neighboring Granada was tributary to the king of Castile, a continuation of the holy war by the Portuguese called for an invasion of North Africa. Prince Henry led an expedition against Ceuta in 1415 and took it. He regarded this as the beginning of extensive conquests in Morocco in continuation of a war for the faith. But when, in 1437, he tried to take Tangiers, he met with a disaster so crushing that a promise to surrender Ceuta was the price of escape. For Henry such surrender seemed to sacrifice the holy war. So he repudiated his promise even though this meant that his youngest brother, held as a hostage for his good faith, died miserably in a Moorish prison, a martyr to the cause. Henry was determined to crush the Muslim Moors. He was eager to spread the Christian faith, and he conceived the idea of making contact with the Ethiopian Christians and, in alliance with them, striking Islam from the south. Exploration of the west coast of Africa and efforts to sail around the southern coast of that continent, which was erroneously thought to be about half its actual size, stemmed from these plans. When in 1441 a Portuguese captain for the first time brought back some slaves from the west coast of Africa, a new commercial opportunity appeared to challenge the crusading idea, one that would prove too strong to combat. There is irony in the realization that the African slave trade thus seems to be one of the results of the crusades.

For the kings of Castile the presence of Granada, a tributary Moorish state, on their southern border

was neither a danger nor an inconvenience. But when
the marriage of Ferdinand and Isabella brought about
a union of the Spanish kingdoms, a deliberate decision
to perfect this union by conquering Granada followed.
In keeping with Isabella's sincere religious zeal, the
crusading aspect of this conquest was emphasized and
adventurers from Germany, France, and England came
to this new crusade. A Spanish fleet at the Straits of
Gibraltar prevented help from the North African Muslims. Several years of effort closed on January 2, 1492,
when the surrender of Granada completed the Christian reconquest of the Iberian Peninsula—a success
that might seem in some measure to balance the Muslim advance in southeastern Europe. As with the
Portuguese, the zeal for fighting the infidel carried
Spanish armies into North Africa where they made a
series of conquests along the coast as far east as Oran
and Algiers. Cardinal Ximenes urged further conquests
inland as part of an effective crusade against Islam,
but more secularly minded soldiers hesitated. King
Ferdinand's attention was turning to Italy; Queen Isabella was dead. We may properly note that Columbus
had earlier presented himself to the queen in the camp
before Granada. Part of the argument which he advanced to interest the queen was that the gold and
spices he hoped to find would enable the Catholic
kings, within three years, to conquer the Holy
Sepulcher. Las Casas, the historian of the Indies,
pictures Columbus as a man zealous for religion and
eager to spread Christianity among the Indians, and,
continues this author, "he was especially affected and
devoted to the idea that God should deem him worthy
of aiding somewhat in recovering the Holy Sepulcher."
Even the discovery of America, then, has a tenuous link
with the crusades, and the conquistadores appear
vaguely as crusaders extending Christian rule, although
it is hard to accord the crown of martyrdom to those
unfortunate companions of Cortez who were captured
and sacrificed to the Aztec war god.

C H A P T E R . . . 4

The Results
of the Crusades

Cultural Contact of Christian
and Muslim

Three times during the Christian era have the peoples
of Western Europe experienced a relatively rapid
expansion of their knowledge of the world, which has
greatly improved their manner of living and considerably changed their point of view. The first of these
was during the period of the crusades; the second
came in the Renaissance; and the third is that phase
of the Industrial Revolution, the age of science, in
which we now live. It is the first of these that here
engages our attention. But we should not assume that
the crusades themselves were anything more than con-
tributary to these developments of the later Middle
Ages. They are sometimes credited with influences
that cannot be adequately substantiated. Indeed, in con-

sidering the results of the crusades it is proper to review the whole process whereby the Western peoples
learned from the Byzantines and Muslims, both of
whom enjoyed civilizations founded upon the culture
of the classical Roman Empire. This educational process was already begun when Urban preached at Clermont, and would undoubtedly have taken place, more
slowly perhaps and somewhat differently, had there
been no great military pilgrimages to the Holy Land.
Those expeditions stimulated it, excited a curiosity in
new things among tens of thousands of persons, and
provided them with an opportunity for learning about
the world—a most potent civilizing influence.

It must always be remembered, however, that those
undertakings merely established new points of contact
with the older civilizations. Already, in Spain, Christian
and Muslim had been living side by side since the
eighth century. The warfare of conquest and reconquest was intermittent, but even at its worst it did not
prevent considerable mingling of peoples. Both parties tolerated their opponents of the opposite faith
when territory was annexed; Christian scholars could
and did go to the Muslim universities; and always the
Jews provided intermediaries between Moorish Spain
and the north. Again in Sicily, which the Normans of
southern Italy conquered from the Saracens in the
eleventh century, occurred a mingling of Latins, Byzantines, and Muslims productive of a flourishing culture
accessible to Italy, France, England, and Germany.
The Sicilian kings and the early Italian republics had
established commercial relations with North Africa,
Constantinople, and Muslim Spain before the end of
the eleventh century; these trade ideas continued even
after Europe focused on Syria.

Commercial Contact with Syria

When the men of the First Crusade settled in Syria,
they and their successors had to depend upon Europe

for certain necessary supplies, horses, armor, cloth, and the like, which gave occasion for a trade that grew with great rapidity. But the more important trade, as viewed from Italian counting houses, once Eastern emporia were established, was with the Muslims, particularly the Egyptians. Whether or not further crusading would advance or retard such trade at any particular time would be uncertain. European products such as timber, arms, and slaves, desired by the Egyptians, were regarded as munitions of war, but repeated denunciation of selling such exports to the Muslims in the interests of crusading were ineffective. The clergy found they could more easily arouse enthusiasm for the holy war among the feudal nobility and the common people than in Italian commercial circles. Traders did business where they thought to find profits, either with popes, crusaders, or sultans. Trade with Egypt and Syria continued and flourished after crusading to the East stopped; so did pilgrimage, but not on such a large scale as before.

Pilgrims who returned from the East brought back a knowledge of new products, which they had learned to enjoy during their stay in foreign parts. In this way new demands and new markets were created in the West of which enterprising merchants sought to avail themselves. The introduction into Europe of new articles of commerce, new natural products, and new commercial practices by way of this Muslim trade is clearly marked by the words borrowed from the Arabic which appear during the crusading epoch. Cotton, muslin (cloth of Mosul), and damask (cloth of Damascus) became recognized and important articles of commerce. New vegetables and fruits, known among the Muslim peoples, appeared, such as rice, sugar, lemons, apricots (sometimes called Damascus plums), and garlic (shalot, that is, little onions of Ascalon).

Under the pressure of a growing commerce well-defined trade routes, by land and sea, but particularly in the Mediterranean, came to be established. The cru-

sades recovered for Christendom the naval control of
the Mediterranean Sea lost since the ninth century.
European sailors need no longer timidly hug the shores
of the Balkan Peninsula, carrying on a limited trade
with Constantinople. They could dare to make directly for Syria, Egypt, and the North African coast,
learning by experience the art of navigation in Mediterranean waters. Northerners, like the English in the
reign of Richard the Lion-Hearted, undertook naval
expeditions on a scale larger than they had ever before
attempted and came in contact with the Byzantine,
Muslim, and Italian traditions and practices of navigation and ship-building. Trade required vessels of
large capacity and cheap propulsion. The result was
the development of sailing ships large enough to carry
800 to 1000 persons, but very slow moving because
entirely dependent upon the wind. One of these in
the thirteenth century would require eight weeks to
make the trip from the Levant to Western Europe
that an ordinary steamer now makes in five days. By
the twelfth century, knowledge of the compass had
been learned, probably from the East, but not from
the Muslims, and navigators were using magnetized
needles attached to straws or splinters and floating in
water as a means for determining direction. The importance of this simple contrivance to maritime development can scarcely be overemphasized. At the
same time a Muslim instrument, the astrolabe, became
known and used for determining latitude, thus en-
abling a ship captain to ascertain his position. The increased experience of large numbers of European sailors
made possible the collection of the vast amount of
detailed geographical knowledge which is necessary for
map-making, and the needs of navigators stimulated
such manufacture, so that by the end of the crusading
epoch relatively accurate maps of the Mediterranean
had already been made. All these things arising from
the crusades were helping to encourage a new economic
development for Western Europe, a development based

on commerce rather than on agricultural pursuits.

A corollary of this revival of commerce was the return of Europe to a money economy such as had characterized the Roman Empire. This had begun before the eleventh century and would have come eventually had there been no crusades, but the rapid growth of the Levantine trade, and the movement of thousands of travelers brought speedily to an end the period of barter, and substituted a period of money and credit. This can, perhaps, be illustrated by the reappearance of gold coins among the west Europeans. In the early Middle Ages gold was too valuable to be coined. There were no transactions requiring pieces worth so much. Among the Byzantines and Muslims, where business flourished, gold coins remained in use, and it is those parts of Europe which first took part in the Eastern trade and came into commercial relations with the Saracens and the Eastern Empire, which during the crusading period developed enough business to warrant the minting of gold. The kings of Sicily took the lead,[1] but the Italian cities were the ones who reintroduced the practice effectively. In 1252 appeared the first florins (that is, coins of Florence); the Venetian sequin came a generation later; and similar coins in the rest of Europe soon followed. But long before this date the large transactions resulting from the crusading movement had brought about a system of international banking. Barons and princes who wished to go crusading found themselves in need of large sums which they sought to get by selling or mortgaging their lands, or by borrowing. On a smaller scale this was true of every pilgrim. The result was an enormous business in money. But to carry all one's wealth from the Rhine to the Jordan was both dangerous and inconvenient. Furthermore, as trade between the East and West

[1] The first gold coins in the West since the Carolingians were struck by Roger II (1130–1154) as duke of Apulia, hence the name ducat. Frederick II revived the imperial solidi of Constantine and Theodosius.

grew, the settlement of large transactions in coin was
similarly cumbersome. There was a real need for de-
vising some means of exchange whereby the transport
of gold and silver could be avoided or reduced to a min-
imum. The Templars, as we have seen, carried on a
system of international banking. The would-be pilgrim could deposit his money in the "temple" in Paris
and receive a receipt, a letter of credit, which enabled
him to obtain money for his journey to the Holy Land
and back from the different chapters of the order en
route. Similarly Western merchants, buying goods in
the East, paid for the same with orders on the "temple"
in Jerusalem. The Italians, who, in the course of trade,
established offices and correspondents throughout the
East, were not slow to imitate the Templars in carrying on this profitable business in money. It was the
beginning of modern international banking.

The initial success of the crusaders and the profits
accruing from the Levantine trade served also as stim-
uli for further penetration of Asia on the part of bold
merchants. It seems probable that some Italian traders made their way from the Syrian coast into the interior toward Bagdad, the greatest emporium of western
Asia. Still more probable is it that commercial relations with the Egyptians introduced Europeans to the
Red Sea route to the Far East, although it may be
doubted if any reached the eastern parts of Asia by
water. The Muslims enjoyed the position of middlemen in these regions between Europe and Asia, successfully excluding the Europeans from contact with the
sources of Oriental trade. Most important results,
however, followed from the capture of Constantinople
in 1204. This opened to the Venetians all the possibilities of the Black Sea trade, which they were not slow
to realize. Establishing themselves on its northern and
eastern shores, they pushed into Russia and south of
the Caucasus toward Central Asia. The Mongol attack upon the Turks and the Caliphate of Bagdad, and
the hope that it inspired among the Christians of an

alliance against the common foe, provided another occasion for the Westerners to get in touch with the farther parts of Asia. It was repeatedly rumored that the
Great Khan desired to be converted to Christianity.
Consequently, kings and popes sent envoys to the Tartars by the overland routes through Russia and Tur-
kestan, Venetian merchants—of whom the Polos are the
outstanding examples—penetrated the Mongol empire
in search of trade, and Christian missionaries drawn
from the mendicant orders sought to spread the Gos-
pel among these distant heathen. The result was the
discovery of Asia, the acquisition of a mass of informa-
tion about that continent and its resources that so en-
larged the European horizon and stimulated the desire
for trade relations direct with the Far East.

But like the crusading movement, from which these
activities sprung, they were all doomed to failure. The
Tartars not only did not become converted to Christianity, they eventually became Muslims. Their empire
fell to pieces, and all hope of obtaining their alliance
against the Turks faded. These facts, coupled with the
collapse of the Latin states in Syria and the increased
geographical knowledge of Asia, suggested to some
Europeans that, inasmuch as they could not control
the land routes of western Asia in the face of a triumphant Islam, they might possibly discover a sea route
to the Far East and so free themselves from the
Muslim middlemen. The advocates of new crusades in
the later thirteenth century, when the Latin Kingdom
was rapidly approaching its end, insisted that trade
with the Muslims must be stopped as a necessary
preliminary for conducting the holy war. This would
ruin Egypt, since the time of Saladin the chief enemy
for the crusaders. The possibility of circumnavigating
Africa seems to have originated with certain of these
enthusiasts toward the end of the century. It was in
1270 that the Genoese first essayed Atlantic exploration
and rediscovered the Canary Islands, and in 1291, the
very year of the fall of Acre, that two Genoese galleys

sailed out to find the route to India and to bring
back useful merchandise. They were never heard of
again, but they form one of the connecting links between the commercial enterprise of the crusading period
and the age of discoveries.

Effects of the Crusades upon Western Society

In regard to the social and political influence of the
crusades it is necessary to be cautious lest too many
of the changes which took place in Europe during the
twelfth and thirteenth centuries be ascribed to their
influence. That feudal society was in a process of slow
transformation, that politically national monarchies
were gradually beginning to form, and the international
ecclesiastical system to show signs of decay, is obvious
quite apart from the crusades. The latter merely contributed to those changes—probably hastening them—
by increasing the movement of large numbers of
people, which usually tends to stimulate change. The
idea that these wars and pilgrimages diminished the
population does not seem to be borne out by demo-
graphic studies.[2] Considering the probable life ex-
pectancy of medieval men, it may well be that crusading
made no notable statistical difference. Crusading did
provide an opportunity for the man who found living
hard (and who in the Middle Ages did not?) and who
possessed sufficient enterprise, to begin life again. If
he were in debt assuming the cross relieved him, for
the moment at least, of the burden of his obligations by
giving him a moratorium; if he were an outlaw he received a pardon, and the expedition to Syria assured
him of salvation in heaven and the possibility of material gain upon earth. Pious lords, concerned for their

[2] A chapter on "Demography of the Crusades" is scheduled for
one of the later volumes of *The History of the Crusades,* edited
by K. Setton.

souls' welfare often freed their serfs as a preliminary to their departure, or, needing money for their pilgrimage, sold emancipation. These facts, combined with the trade revival that came from the crusades, aided in the growth of industry and the more rapid development of town life. Such changes, once started, reacted on each other. More freemen, no longer bound to an agricultural existence, meant the development of handicrafts at which they could make a profitable living by trade. Their life attracted the serfs of the vicinity, and the desire for freedom became greater. The demand became more insistent until, by a gradual process, the unfree agricultural laborer became a peasant tenant farmer or a townsman.

On the other hand, the losses of the crusading war fell most heavily upon the feudal nobility, particularly in France. Financial needs might lead to the sale or mortgage of part of their lands, often effecting a permanent change of ownership. Heirs died on the road to the East, or in warfare with the Muslims, or settled permanently in Syria. The noble class as a whole lost both in wealth and personnel by its active participation in the holy war, and this resulted in diminishing its political and military importance. In France, consequently, where the nobility took so large a part in the crusades, we find the king profiting by this preoccupation of his strongest political rivals and increasing the power and wealth of the throne at their expense, while in England and Germany, where the nobility took less interest in the holy war, the monarch continued to find an effective check in the baronage. In this connection should be noted the levying of general contributions in money to meet the expenses of crusading, which may be considered the beginning of royal taxation. The earliest of these is in 1146, and the most famous is the "Saladin tithe" of 1188. Similarly, the pope demanded money from the clergy, a practice which became a precedent and often was delegated to different kings.

Effects of the Crusades
upon the Western Church

If the newly developing monarchies profited most
from the crusades, politically speaking, probably the
oldest institution of medieval Europe, the papacy,
suffered most heavily. At the start, it benefited by the
crusades through which it appeared as the leader of
Europe during the twelfth century. But the Fourth
Crusade demonstrated that even Innocent III could
not control the movement, and the subsequent failure
and misuse of crusading for selfish political purposes
seriously discredited the papacy. In the thirteenth
century, when the holy war against the Muslims was
permitted to lag while "crusades" were preached and
waged against the Hohenstauffen in Italy, the popes
were blamed for sttirring up war among Christians,
for embezzling funds collected for the war against the
Muslims, for preferring the dynastic ambitions of their
French allies to the recovery of the Holy Land, and for
perverting from the East to Europe, merely for local,
political reasons, the military strength that might
have saved Jerusalem. The Muslim victories were regarded as the judgment of God upon the Christians,
and the blame was laid upon the popes. Subsequent
pontiffs in the fifteenth century sought to revive crusading ardor against the Turks, but the papacy had
been too much discredited by that date, and its authority had too much declined, for it to be able to
rekindle the religious zeal of 1095, even when the
danger in Europe from the Turk was very real. Too
often the popes were suspected of utilizing a crusade
as a political expedient and as an excuse for levying
taxes. The pontiffs themselves came to regard the suppression of heretics in Europe as more important than
combating the infidels. In the sixteenth century, the
wars of religion between Catholics and Protestants
could satisfy any urge to wage holy wars at papal instigation.

At the same time the crusades helped to break down church discipline, one of the fundamentals of the ecclesiastical system. Through the sacrament of penance the Church sought to bring the erring to repentance and to the expiation of the temporal punishment due to sin. For the ordinary layman this was the means whereby the Church exercised authority over his daily life and sought to make him conform to Christian standards. From the tenth century this temporal punishment was sometimes remitted, in whole or in part, through the granting of indulgence to an individual who performed some particularly pious act. Plenary indulgences, the remission of all penances, were among the means of persuading warriors to assume the cross, and the difficulties and dangers of the holy war could very properly be regarded as the equivalent of all penance. But the issuance of indulgences suffered the same discrediting misuse as the crusade itself, when war against the heretics in Languedoc, or the Hohenstauffen, or rebellious barons of the papal states came to be considered "crusades." And it was an easy development from this to the sale of pardons. Originally, when a man took the crusader's vow he must make his pilgrimage to the Holy Land or be excommunicated. If for good reason he could not perform his vow, the pope could release him from it, but in such case it seemed only proper that he should contribute toward the holy war in commutation of his unperformed vow. From this, as the financial needs of the papacy increased, it was not difficult to use the release from crusading vows as a source of revenue, and as crusaders enjoyed indulgences their sale became a recognized means of raising money, first for the holy war, and then for any papal need. Eventually this practice led to Luther's protest.

Civilization under the Caliphs

Inasmuch as Europe borrowed extensively from the Muslims in matters intellectual during the period of the crusades, it is desirable to reconsider the nature of Saracen culture and something of its content. The most flourishing period of that culture had passed before the crusades began, but Muslim society in the eleventh and following centuries still enjoyed the civilization developed under the great caliphs, particularly in Egypt and Spain.

The regions that the Arabs first conquered had enjoyed a flourishing culture long before Muhammad. Syria and Egypt had been centers of the Hellenistic world since the days of Alexander the Great. Persia had inherited a national civilization of great antiquity and was in touch with India and the East. The Arab conquerors themselves represented no great intellectual strength, but under the stimulus of Islam they developed a political virility that, blending with the old Greco-Persian culture, produced in the eighth and ninth centuries a brilliant renaissance of art, learning, and science.

Conditions were favorable for such a development. The income of the Muslim empire was at the disposal of the autocratic caliph. This enabled the rulers at Bagdad, and later at Cordova and Cairo, to become lavish patrons of art and learning, bestowing the wealth of the state upon scholars, poets, and scientists. Like most enlightened despots, the caliphs undertook to make their rule glorious by magnificent building projects and the discriminating patronage of genius. To this policy their subjects responded enthusiastically. The Arabs, even during the conquest, had always recognized the superiority of the culture that they encountered in the lands which they overran. In contrast to the Germans, who barbarized the Roman civilization of Western Europe, the Muslims exhibited an intellectual adaptability which enabled them to turn with understanding to the philosophy and science of antiquity. Muslims enjoyed a greater intellectual freedom during the Middle Ages than did the Christians. It is true that the most rigidly orthodox theologians frowned

upon the study of science and philosophy; but they did
not form an organized priesthood dominating the intellectual life of the community, consequently their influence could not check the scientific investigations which
the caliphs, themselves the religious heads of Islam,
encouraged. Freethinking, often quite infidel in its
character, and with it scientific inquiry, flourished under the Abbassid caliphs. Nor was Islam overbur-
dened with an ascetic ideal which looked with disfavor
upon all worldly enjoyment. For the Muslim, salvation did not require mortification of the flesh. On the
contrary, Muhammad had achieved prosperity for the
faithful as well as assurance of blissful eternity. This
ideal of enjoyment had developed a love of luxury
that, when refined by Persian influences, formed the
basis of Saracen civilization. The believer was free to
indulge his intellectual and artistic tastes, and to apply
himself with enthusiasm to the study of natural science
with a view to obtaining practical results. Furthermore,
the policy of tolerance toward unbelievers gave the
Muslims the opportunity to learn from Christian and
Jewish scholars whom the caliphs patronized as readily
as they did their own coreligionists. In such conditions
there grew up prosperous cities, an active industry and
commerce, and a keen intellectual life in which the
leaders were usually physicians and astronomers, men
who were practical investigators by profession.

It early became the policy of the Abbassid caliphs to
encourage scientific study on the basis of the Greek
classics. The Caliph Harun al-Rashid (786–809) ordered
the works of Aristotle and of the Greek physicians
Hippocrates and Galen translated from the Syriac into
Arabic. It is said that on his travels he was always
accompanied by a hundred learned men, and he de-
creed that whenever a mosque was built a school should
be attached to it. He even appointed a Christian to
superintend the schools of the caliphate. His son al-
Mamun (813–833) sent special commissions to Constantinople and to India to obtain copies of as many

scientific works as possible, and at one time he made the surrender of a large number of Greek manuscripts one of the conditions of peace for the emperor. Of this caliph a Muslim chronicler relates:

> He was not ignorant that they are the elect of God—His best and most useful servants—whose lives are devoted to the improvement of their rational faculties.—The teachers of wisdom are the true luminaries and legislators of the world, which, without their aid. would again sink into ignorance and barbarism.

Arab-Greek and Arab-Latin dictionaries were compiled to enable the Saracen savants to study the ancient authors in the original and to make their own translations, and works on mathematics, astronomy, medicine, and philosophy in great numbers were published in Arabic. At Bagdad was founded the "House of Science," a learned academy manned by a corps of translators and learned men, and equipped with a library and an observatory. Similar foundations, veritable universities with laboratories and libraries of secular and scientific as well as religious books, centers of research and publication as well as instruction, appeared in other parts of the Muslim world also. Since Muhammad had forbidden his followers to translate his relevations into any other tongue than Arabic, the language of the Koran provided Islam with a linguistic bond that made the exchange of books and ideas throughout the Muslim world easy and gave a cultural unity to Saracen civilization despite the political disunion. The Umayyad caliphs in Spain established institutions of learning like those of Bagdad at Cordova and Toledo, and the Fatimids did likewise at Cairo. The versatility and productivity of some of the learned Muslims suggests the Italian Renaissance of the fifteenth century. One Cordovan scholar is credited with 1100 works on metaphysics, history, and medicine. "There are two creatures that are insatiable," said a Muslim proverb, "the man

of money and the man of science"; and another saying
declared that "the ink of the learned is as precious
as the blood of the martyrs."

Arabic Astronomy

Perhaps the oldest science to which the Saracens devoted themselves was the study of the heavens. The
region which formed the nucleus of the Bagdad Caliphate was that in which, during Hellenistic times,
Greco-Babylonian astronomy had been most flourishing. The ancient astronomers and their Saracen successors were primarily astrologers, but it would be a
mistake, on that account, to regard them as pseudo-
scientists. They assumed that there were natural laws
whereby the heavenly bodies influenced human affairs,
and they strove by observation of the stars, by careful
record of astronomical facts and of the events which
followed to discover the working of those laws. Furthermore the Greeks, whose system the Saracens appropriated, in their effort to plumb the depths of astro-
logical lore, had associated the heavenly bodies, on the
one hand with the various gods of their pantheon and,
on the other hand, with everything to do with the life
of man, days of the week,[3] colors, minerals, animals,
plants, and drugs. Consequently astrology led to the
study, not only of astronomy, but also of mineralogy,
zoology, botany, chemistry, and medicine.[4]

The Abbassid translators had made available the
works of Ptolemy on geography and astronomy (the
latter indeed is still known by its Arabic name *Almagest*), and Hindu works on the same subjects were
similarly translated. Under the caliphs' patronage, observatories were established in the principal cities.
Here were installed scientific instruments, often of

[3] The names of the days, which we still employ, originated
with the pagan astrologers.
[4] The mark, still used for medical prescriptions, is the astro-
logical symbol for Jupiter.

great size, made with unusual skill, from some of which
modern surveying instruments have been developed.[5]
By studying the Ptolemaic and Hindu theories and records and making observations of their own, the Saracen astronomers proved again many of the ancient theories and made new discoveries. They constructed
astronomical tables showing the orbits of the planets,
which the king of Castile imitated in the thirteenth
century. They catalogued the stars more thoroughly
than Ptolemy had done so that many of the Arabic
names for important stars (Aldebaran, Althair, Rigel,
Vega) have become established in modern astronomy.
By careful observation one Saracen astronomer in the
ninth century determined the length of the year more
correctly than had been done under Julius Caesar
whose calendar prevailed in Western Europe until modern times, while a second astronomer in the eleventh
century reformed the calendar with even greater exact-
ness than was done under Pope Gregory XIII, whose
system is now observed by Europeans. The precise
prohibitions of the Prophet against any alteration of
the calendar prevented the application of these discoveries to practical daily use, and the Muslim world still
reckons time according to the lunar year. The angle of
the sun's ecliptic and the precession of the equinoxes
were determined with considerable accuracy. The phenomenon of the sun's movement among the stars, which
is the basis for the modern theory that the solar system
itself is moving through space, was observed but
wrongly interpreted. The third inequality of the moon,
the variation, namely, that the moon moves most
quickly when new or full and slowest in its first and
third quarters, was discovered by Saracens six hundred
years before European astronomers. By astronomical
means longitude and latitude were computed; the latitude of Bagdad was established within ten seconds;

[5] The astrolabe and alidade are instruments perfected by the
Saracens. Such words as azimuth, zenith, and nadir have come
into our language from Saracen astronomy.

tables were published showing the longitude and latitude of the chief places in the Muslim world; and the
caliph al-Mamun sent out two parties of scientists to
measure on a level plain in Mesopotamia a degree on
the earth's surface, an experiment not attempted in
western Europe for a thousand years.

Arabic Mathematics

For the Saracens, as for the Greeks and Hindus before them, the science of mathematics was auxiliary to
astronomy, and most of the great Muslim mathematicians were primarily astronomers. Among the Greeks
and Romans, and following them the medieval Europeans, the study of mathematics and its practical application was hampered by the character of the symbols,
which was such as to make computation a necessarily
clumsy process. Letters of the Greek alphabet, con-
ventionalized fingers (I. II. III.), or initial letters (C
for *centum*, M for *mille*) were used. This made arithmetic difficult and calculation with very large numbers
practically impossible.[6] A mechanical device, the abacus,
was necessary for figuring with such arbitrary symbols.
To the Saracens the Western world is indebted for
the "Arabic numerals," which they in turn had learned
from the Hindus. In the nine digits themselves there
is no peculiar virtue. Like the Greek letters they are
merely conventional signs which may have been known
in western Europe in the early Middle Ages. What
makes the Hindu-Arabic numerals so important in the
history of science is the addition of the zero [7] and the
application of the principle of position to arithmetic.
In the ninth century we find the numerals utilized
in the standard Arabic works on mathematics by

[6] Imagine, for instance, doing complicated problems with the
Egyptian symbol for a million, the hieroglyph of a man expressing great astonishment.

[7] This word, cipher, and the French *chiffre* are all derived
from the Arabic word which was probably a corruption of the
Hindu word for "void, empty."

means of which they eventually found their way into Europe in the twelfth century.

Among the Europeans of the later Middle Ages arithmetic with the Hindu-Arabic numerals, as distinguished from computation by means of the abacus, was called "algorism." This is a corruption of the name of the most distinguished of the Saracen mathematicians, al-Khwarizmi, an astronomer of the early ninth century, contemporary with Harun al-Rashid, and an extensive writer on arithmetic, the sun-dial, the astrolabe, chronology, geometry, and algebra. Indeed, in addition to the new numerals, it is from one of his works that not only the fundamentals of that mathematical science but also the very name "algebra" is derived; [8] and from the same book other permanent mathematical conceptions such as "root" and "power" have been borrowed. His work also serves to illustrate the practical point of view of the Saracens, for al-Khwarizmi describes his Algebra as a work which seeks to provide the easiest and more useful method of calculation "such as men constantly require in cases of inheritance, legacies, partition, law-suits, and trade, and in all their dealings with one another, or where the measuring of lands, the digging of canals, geometrical computation, and other objects of various sorts and kinds are concerned."

Furthermore, in mathematics as in other sciences the Arabic translators were the means for transmitting to western Europe the works of the ancients such as Euclid's *Elements of Geometry* and the studies in trigonometry in Ptolemy's *Almagest*. The Saracen contribution to the ancient stock of learning in these subjects was not so distinguished as in arithmetic and

---

[8] "Al-gebr we'l mukabala," meaning "restoration and opposition" and referring, the one to the transposition of negative terms to the other side of the equation ($8x-3y = 13 + 4x$ becoming $8x = 13 + 4x + 3y$), and the other to the discarding of like terms from both. sides of the equation ($8x = 13 + 4x + 3y$ becoming $4x = 13 + 3y$).

algebra but it is nevertheless, noteworthy. They applied algebra, an easier method, to propositions where the Greeks had resorted to geometry. They discovered the geometric solution of cubic equations. In trigonometry they made improvement by introducing the sine, borrowed from the Hindus, for the whole chord of Ptolemy. They developed the study of conic sections and calculated a table of tangents, finally succeeding in divorcing trigonometry from astronomy and making it a pure science in itself.

Arabic Chemistry

In the experimental sciences the Saracens were also proficient, notably in alchemy, another word borrowed by Europeans from the Muslims along with much of the science which it denotes. According to the ancient Greek philosophers, all metals are composed, fundamentally, of the same elements. Their differences are merely matters of proportion. Consequently it was assumed that, by resolving metals into their elements and by then recombining those elements in the proper proportions the scientist could produce in his laboratory whatever metal he desired. This search by the Saracen alchemists for the formula for transmutation whereby lead and iron could be changed into gold and silver led to extensive experimentation. It was supposed that a substance existed that would not only have the desired effect upon metals, but would also completely cure all disease including old age. Needless to say, the alchemists never discovered the secret of transmutation, the philosopher's stone, nor the elixir of life, but they did discover many valuable scientific facts which have become the basis for modern chemistry. The Saracen acquaintance with alcohol and alkalis is indicated by the words themselves, and knowledge of sal ammoniac, corrosive sublimate, silver nitrate, and red precipitate resulted from Muslim experimentation. The mixing of "noble" and "base" metals in the search for transmutation taught the alchemists how to make alloys and amalgams, and to determine the specific gravity of some of the important elements.

Arabic Medicine

Besides the observatories and libraries which the government established, the caliphs also endowed hospitals, which were not only places where the sick received treatment, but were also institutions of learning where the practice of medicine was taught and medical research carried on. In order to determine the most salubrious site for one of these foundations, it is said that the caliph's chief physician hung pieces of meat in different parts of Bagdad. After some time these were examined and the hospital located at the place where putrefaction had been the slowest. The works of Hippocrates and Galen formed the basis for Arab medicine, particularly for the study of anatomy, for Islam abhorred the dissection of the human body. Anatomical research, however, was conducted with animals. But the Saracens were students of medicine rather than of surgery. They notably increased the pharmacopoeia by their experiments with useful drugs, handing on to Christian Europe a knowledge of senna, aconite, rhubarb, nux vomica, and camphor. In contrast with contemporary Christian physicians, the Saracens regarded disease as a natural phenomenon rather than the expression of the malevolence of devils or of the wrath of God. Their medical works describe diseases and symptoms with careful detail, recount methods of treatment and record the results obtained from them. In this way the Saracens, by observation and experiment, became expert on matters of hygiene and diet as well as in the administration of drugs.[9] They knew how to use alcohol in treating disease, and even psychology was not neglected, for professional entertainers

[9] Our words elixir, syrup, julep, and sherbet have been borrowed from Saracen medicine.

were attached to the hospitals to cheer the melancholiacs and to amuse those who suffered from insomnia.

The Works of Aristotle

Among the most precious of the ancient works that the Syrian heretics introduced to the Muslims were the writings of Aristotle. His philosophical and scientific books had been translated into Syriac and extensively commented upon before the rise of Islam, and their translation into Arabic in the eighth and ninth centuries was merely a part of the Abbassid renaissance of learning. The decline of the old religious fervor of Islam was favorable to the study of Aristotelian philosophy, which is essentially materialistic and logical. But rationalism of this sort very easily led to skepticism and freethinking of a wholly unorthodox character. The theologians were hostile to philosophical speculation, and the populace, always devout and intellectually conservative, was sometimes excited to violence against the philosophers. But the boldness of the Saracen thinkers, protected, as they usually were, by the caliphs, caused Aristotelianism to flourish among the Muslims until the twelfth century, when Christian Europe was ready to renew the study of the greatest of the ancient thinkers.

For the Saracens, Aristotle was the founder and the perfecter of all scientific knowledge and speculation. Beyond him the human intelligence could not go. They attempted to imitate him by accepting his fundamental doctrines and adopting his method of logical reasoning by means of definition and the syllogism. Like him they essayed to understand all the sciences, to achieve encyclopedic knowledge, and to develop a complete rational system. Such ambitions, whatever philosophical success they achieved, vigorously stimulated the investigating, skeptical spirit which is the essence of intellectual vitality. Most Muslim philosophers, consequently, were physicians and scientists as well as abstract

thinkers. Of these the last and greatest, Averroës
(1126–1198), lived in Spain. His commentary first
introduced the whole of Aristotle's writing to
Christian Europe. He also serves tᴏ illustrate the extent of Muslim free thought, for by the twelfth century the Saracen thinkers had been forced to accept the
divorce of science and religion. Aristotle was essentially a rationalist and materialist, and in following him
Averroës and others had had to deny the possibility of
creation in the orthodox sense, recognizing instead the
indestructibility of matter and the principle of evolution. An appreciation of the workings of natural law
led them to reject the idea of Divine Providence or interference of God in the lives of individuals, while their
pantheistic conceptions in regard to the intellect, both
universal and particular, were contradictory to the doctrines of the resurrection and the immortality of the
soul. No man, according to Averroës, attains to any
reward other than his own virtue. But such conclu-
sions were more than even the Muslim community
would tolerate. Averroës marks the end of liberal science in Muslim Spain.

Transmission of Saracen Culture through Spain and Sicily

Among the most important consequences of Christian contact with the Muslims was the vast increase in
scientific knowledge which came from the translation
into Latin of the learned works written by Arabic scholars, and this resulted much more from conditions in
Spain and Sicily than from the establishment of the
Latin Kingdom of Jerusalem. Throughout the early
Middle Ages, Moorish Spain had been recognized by
Christian scholars as a center of learning worth visiting
despite the dangers of travel and the difficulties of understanding Arabic. The latter, being a Semitic language, presented a great obstacle to easy translation

because of its marked differences from the European
tongues. The northern scholar must remain a long
time in a foreign land before he could understand both
the language and the science well enough to attempt
translation. Probably, in Spain, the Jews were utilized
as instructors and assistants. We can imagine some
English student, after learning the vernacular spoken
by the Christian population in Toledo, making friends
with some learned Jew who knew Arabic. The latter
would translate a scientific or philosophical book into
the vernacular, and the Christian would then translate
it again into Latin. Technical terms, for which no
Latin equivalent existed, would merely be transliter-
ated. As this was often a word-by-word translation, the
general form, even after the sentences had been made
to conform to the rules of Latin grammar, remained
Arabic, which often made the book difficult to understand for the readers beyond the Pyrenees. The labo-
riousness of this process makes intelligible why Arabic learning was introduced only slowly into Europe.
The success of the Spanish reconquest helped this process. In 1085 Toledo was recovered from the Moors.
During the first half of the next century the Archbishop
of Toledo, desiring to make Arabic philosophy available for Christians, organized a college of translators to
render into Latin Muslim works on science and philosophy. Thither came Gerard of Cremona "for the love
of that which he could not find among the Latins,"
namely Ptolemy's *Almagest,* the most important work
of ancient astronomy, and devoted himself to translation; and other adventurous scholars, attracted by the
novelties of Arabic science, and wearied by the "law
and pretentious ignorance" that dominated northern
schools, followed him, eventually to return home
laden with valuable books. In the same half century Adelard of Bath, a man who "sought out the
causes of all things and the mysteries of nature" was
traveling extensively in southern Italy, Sicily, and the

Levant in order to learn the wisdom of the Arabs, returning to Europe with manuscripts on astronomy and
mathematics, which he translated into Latin.

Second only to the schools of Toledo in transmitting
eastern learning was the court of the Norman kings of
Sicily at Palermo. These rulers, who had established
themselves in the island only a short time before the
First Crusade, were tolerant toward the mixed population, Greek, Jewish, and Saracen, of the island, and
from the start followed an enlightened policy of adapt-
ing themselves to the flourishing civilization which they
found there. Their geographical position brought them
in touch with the Muslims of North Africa and Spain,
while their ambitions to make conquests in the Eastern
Empire led to extensive political relations with Constantinople. King Roger II (1130–1154) was an active
patron of learning and his successors maintained the
cultural tradition throughout the twelfth and thirteenth
centuries. Here flourished a refined court life accus-
tomed to the use of luxuries prevalent in Muslim and
Byzantine countries, which served as an example for
northern Italy. The use of sugar was common, the
growing of cotton and the weaving of silk prevailed,
and it seems highly probable that Sicily was the chan-
nel through which a knowledge of paper-making
reached Europe. In some respects, Palermo was more
favorably placed than Toledo because it was in direct relations with the Byzantines and could obtain
copies of books in the original Greek instead of in
Arabic translations, and we know that manuscripts
were sent from the imperial court to the Norman kings.
The latter, however, did not neglect to send scholars
from their court to Spain to bring back copies of the
works studied there. The scientific spirit of Arabic
learning seems to have appealed to these practical Normans, who showed great interest in worldly knowledge
and the study of nature. It was for Roger II that the
Muslim geographer al-Idrisi, a refugee from Spain and

North Africa, made a celestial sphere and a silver map of the known world that so excited the king's interest that he commissioned men to go out from his court to travel and record their observations of foreign countries in order that al-Idrisi might write a new geography. This he did under the title of *The going out of a Curious Man to explore the Regions of the Globe.*

With Roger's grandson, Emperor Frederick II, a century later, the Sicilian court reached its apogée as a center of culture. Frederick, for political reasons, was a crusader to Jerusalem, but he preferred diplomacy to fighting, even in the war for the faith, gaining his objective by treaty, and utilized the opportunity to cultivate friendly relations with the sultan of Egypt and to gratify his interest in Muslim learning and luxury. He was a great admirer of Arabic philosophy, and an ardent student of natural history. Himself a scholar and a student, he encouraged translators, sending men from his court to study at Toledo and to bring back scientific works, and founding the University of Naples in 1224 for the purpose of introducing Arabic science to the Western world. Among others he patronized Leonard of Pisa whose *Book of the Abacus* was one of the important and effective means of introducing the use of Arabic numerals to Europe.[10] Frederick indeed was so absorbed in worldly learning and so sympathetic toward the Arab philosophers, whom the Church regarded with suspicion, that many of his contemporaries branded him as a freethinker, scornful of all religion, and considered by some to be the Antichrist. He was the forerunner of the age that was coming and for which Greek science and philosophy in a Muslim form were preparing the way.

[10] These numerals had become known to the learned world through Spain before this time. Roger II had used them on some of his coins.

Cultural Influences
from the Crusading States

To what extent the new contacts between East and West resulting directly from the crusades influenced Western civilization is somewhat obscure. It seems possible that the first Western knowledge of Aristotle in the original Greek was one of the consequences of the Latin capture of Constantinople in 1204. Manuscripts may well have been part of the booty which found its way to France after the sack of the city, although relics and precious metals were the articles of particular interest to the crusaders on that occasion. At any rate, shortly after this date Latin scholars give evidence of knowing some non-Arabic writings of the great philosopher. It is highly probable, however, that a large mass of irreplaceable classical Greek literature perished at this time in the wanton destruction attendant upon the city's capture. When in 1438 the desperate Greek emperor came to the Council of Ferrara to bargain for papal assistance in resisting the Turks, Greek scholars accompanied him. Some of them remained in Italy contributing to that already awakened interest in the Greek classics and language which played such an important part in the Renaissance revival of learning.

The influence of Syria seems to have been largely upon costume and military practice, with possible exceptions in regard to certain plants, and the use of windmills. The growing of beards and the wearing of flowing robes over armor were eastern styles adopted by the crusaders. The terminology of heraldry is drawn in part from Arabic and Byzantine sources, the first use of heraldic devices is in the period between the Second and Third crusades, and the necessity for coats of arms may well have resulted from the heterogeneous and international character of the crusading armies. It is in military architecture, however, that the influence of Syria upon the West is most apparent. The elaborate defenses of such a place as Antioch were novelties to the Latins, the advantages of which they were quick to grasp. Here was a phase of the architectural greatness of the Roman Empire, preserved and developed by the Byzantines, which made a practical appeal to the feudal mind. The conquerors of Syria undertook to insure their hold on the Levant by building concentric castles with towers strategically placed to command all approaches and all parts of the wall, and crusaders returning to Europe proceeded to imitate these structures when they reached home. Such defenses were usually too much for a feudal army to take by assault, and it was not until the introduction of gunpowder that the age of impregnable fortresses inaugurated by the crusades began to come to an end.

Conclusion

It is from these contacts with Muslim culture and learning that the disintegration of the medieval point of view may be dated. The Europeans learned, in a measure, from what they now knew of the East, to see and appreciate how little the world corresponded to the picture the Church had drawn of it, and how, on the other hand, it supplied a multitude of things that were new, beautiful, and good, and the enjoyment of which they refused longer to forego. And, while enjoying these new pleasures, they overcame many of the prejudices fostered by the Church, and arrived at a state of intellectual and moral independence. In learning from the Muslims, the West added chiefly to its store of knowledge in the fields of mathematics, medicine, alchemy, and astrology, sciences which are founded upon the principles of exact observation of the physical world, and upon the working of immutable natural laws. Such studies eventually proved incompatible with the prevailing religious notions of an omnipotent Creator miraculously intervening in the actions of nature according to his whim and in the interests of his worshippers. Indeed the Muslim thinkers regarded religion merely as something for the uninstructed crowd. Furthermore, scientific study concentrates attention upon the physical world rather than upon eternal life, seeking to make mundane life easier and pleasanter, satisfying human curiosity, and encouraging that lust for knowledge which St. Augustine regarded with horror. The greatest contribution from the Muslim to the Christian world was the complete works of Aristotle. The Saracens prized these highly and commented upon them extensively, and bequeathed their enthusiasm to the Westerners. This is not the place to discuss the influence of Aristotle upon Scholasticism, but it should be noted that the study of his works and those of his Arab commentators, particularly Averroës, may well be considered the first chapter in the history of modern European rationalism and the end of the age of faith.

Bibliographical Note

Of the bibliographical handbooks, L. J. Paetow's *A Guide to the Study of Medieval History for Students, Teachers and Libraries* as revised in 1931 is still standard for works published before that date. It includes works of European scholarship and sources, as well as shorter accounts and text books. Within the last thirty years, however, three notable histories of the crusades have appeared that provide anyone wishing to read widely on this topic with plenty to satisfy his interests. These are: R. Grousset, *Histoire des Croisades et du Royaume Franc de Jérusalem*, 3 vols. (Paris, 1934–1936); Steven Runciman, *A History of the Crusades*, 3 vols. (Cambridge, 1953–1954); and K. M. Setton, ed.-in chief, *A History of the Crusades*, 5 vols. (Philadelphia, 1955ff). Two volumes only of the last named have been published: vol. I, *The First Hundred Years*, ed. by M. W. Baldwin; vol. II, *The Later Crusades, 1189–1311*, ed. by R. L. Wolff (1962). The titles of the other volumes, as announced, are: vol. III, *The Fourteenth and Fifteenth Centuries;* vol. IV, *Civilization and Institutions;* vol. V, *Influences and Consequences,* with genealogies and bibliography. This is a collaborative work, the product of two generations of scholarship. Each of Runciman's volumes has an extensive bibliography — authors and titles — but no comment. Presumably, these lists will give as much guidance to the literature available in 1953 as most readers will want. Runciman's work is both scholarly and readable, but not particularly sympathetic toward crusading. See also A. S. Atiya, *The Crusade in the Later Middle Ages* (London, 1938).

Useful, brief discussions of the crusades, comparable to this present volume, are: E. Barker, *The Crusades* (London.

1923: a reprint of the article in the eleventh edition of the *Encyclopaedia Britannica* 1910–1911); L. Bréhier, *L'Eglise et l'Orient au Moyen Age: Les Croisades* (6th ed; Paris: Bibléothèque de l'enseignment de l'histoire ecclesiastique, 1928); G. G. Coulton, *Crusades, Commerce and Adventure* (London, 1930: Teaching of History Series); J. Longnon, *Les Français d'Outre-Mer au Moyen Age* (2d ed.; Paris, 1929); and H. Treece, *The Crusades* (London, 1962).

For the Byzantine phases of the Christian-Muslim struggle and the Greek relations with the crusaders, consult the *Cambridge Medieval History,* vol. IV, "The Eastern Roman Empire" (Cambridge, 1923). (For the crusades themselves see vol. V [1929]). Standard works of scholarship are G. Schlumberger, *L'Epopée Byzantine à la fin du dixième siècle* (new ed.; Paris, 1925), and the same author's, *Un Empereur Byzantine au dixième siècle; Nicephorus Phocas* (rev. ed.; Paris 1923); F. Chalandon, *Les Comnènes,* 2 vols. (Paris, 1912), and *Histoire de la domination Normand en Italie et en Sicile* 2 vols. (Paris, 1907). Useful general works are A. A. Vasiliev, *History of the Byzantine Empire* (Madison: University of Wisconsin Studies in the Social Sciences and History, no. 13, 1928). This is a translation from the Russian edition of 1917 brought up to date by the author in the process of translation. It contains a selected and critical bibliography of books in all European languages. Attention is also called to L. Bréhier, *Le Monde byzantin,* 3 vols. (Paris: L'Evolution de l'humanité, 1947–1950), and G. Ostrogorsky, *History of the Byzantine Empire* (translated from the German edition of 1952; Oxford, 1956). A highly specialized study confined to a limited but significant field is M. J. Laurent, *Byzance et les Turcs Seldjoucides dans l'Asie Occidentale jusqu'en 1081* (Paris: Annales de l'Est 27ᵉ année, Fascicule I, 1913). This author divides his discussion about evenly between events before and after the battle of Manzikert. He aims to explain the loss of Asia Minor. A briefer, more general discussion is in T. T. Rice, *The Seljuks in Asia Minor* (London: Ancient Peoples and Places Series, no. 2, 1961). See also J. J. Saunders, "The Seljuk Turks and their place in History," with short bibliography, in *History Today,* XII (1962), pp. 336–345.

Attempts at crusader biography should be noted even if, like so many biographies of medieval figures, they tend to be disappointing. These are: C. W. David, *Robert Curthose* (Cambridge, Mass., 1920); R. B. Yewdale, *Bohemond I, Prince of Antioch* (Princeton, 1924); M. W. Baldwin, *Raymond III of Tripolis and the Fall of Jerusalem (1140–1187)* (Princeton, 1936); R. L. Nicholson, *Tancred: A Study of His Career and Work* (Chicago: privately printed, 1940), and *Joscelyn I, Prince of Edessa* (Urbana: Illinois Studies in the Social Sciences, vol. XXXIV, no. 4, 1954), J. C. Andressohn, *The Ancestry and Life of Godfrey of Bouillon* (Bloomington, Ind., 1947); J. H. and L. L. Hill, *Raymond IV de Saint Gilles (1001–1105)* (Toulouse, 1959); G. Schlumberger, *Renaud de Châtillon, prince de Antioch* (Paris, 1898); and R. L. Wolff, "Baldwin of Flanders and Hainaut, First Latin Emperor of Constantinople: His Life, Death and Resurrection, 1172–1225," *Speculum,* XXVII (1952), pp. 281–322. An excellent history of the Third Crusade is in K. Norgate, *Richard the Lion Heart* (London, 1924).

The work of the late Prof. D. C. Munro is of special significance: see particularly his "Christian and Infidel," in *Essays on the Crusades* (Burlington, Vt., 1903); "Speech of Pope Urban II at Clermont, 1095" *(American Historical Review,* XI [1906] pp. 231–242); "The Children's Crusade" *(Ibid.,* XIX [1914] pp. 516–524); "Did the Emperor Alexius Ask for Aid at the Council of Piacenza?" *(Ibid.,* XXVII [1922] pp. 731ff) (On this same subject, see an article by Charles Diehl in *Essays on the Crusades*); "The Popes and the Crusades" *(Proceedings of the American Philosophical Society,* LV [1916], no. 5, p. 1ff); "The establishment of the Latin Kingdom of Jerusalem" *(Sewanee Review,* XXXII [1929], pp. 258ff); "A Crusader" *(Speculum,* VII [1932], no. 3; "The Western Attitude toward Islam during the Period of the Crusades" *(Ibid.,* VI [1931]); *The Kingdom of the Crusaders* (New York, 1935). Also note *The Crusades and Other Historical Essays presented to Dana C. Munro,* L. J. Paetow, ed. (New York, 1928). The collaborative five-volume work cited above grew out of Munro's scholarly teaching.

Many of the sources for the history of the crusades have been translated into English. Notable among these are *The Alexiad* of Anna Comnena (London, 1928), Villehardouin's "Chronicle of the fourth crusade and the conquest of Constantinople" and Joinville's "Chronicle of the crusade of St. Louis." The last two will be found in the Everyman Library volume, *Memoirs of the Crusades* (London, 1908). A guide to translated sources is C. P. Farrar and A. P. Evans, *Bibliography of English Translations from Medieval Sources* (New York: Records of Civilization, no. 39, 1946). This same series includes Pierre Dubois' *The Recovery of the Holy Land,* trans. by W. I. Brandt (*Ibid.,* 1956); Odo of Deuil, *De profectione Ludovic VII in orientem,* trans. by V. G. Berry (*Ibid.,* 1948); and R. S. Lopez and I. Raymond, *Medieval Trade in the Mediterranean World* (*Ibid.,* 1955).

The ideology and the social psychology of crusading is treated in C. Erdmann, *Die Entstehung des Kreuzzugsdanken* (Stuttgart, 1935); P. A. Throop, *Criticism of the Crusades* (Amsterdam, 1940); M. Villey, *La Croisade: Essai sur la formation d'une théorie juridique* (Paris, 1942); P. Rousset, *Les Origines et les Caractères de la Première Croisade;* (Neufchâtel, 1945); and P. Alphandéry, *La Chrétienté et l'Idée de Croisade, Les Premières Croisades; Recommencements Nécessairies (XIIᵉ–XIIIᵉ siècles)* 2 vols. (Paris: L'Evolution de l'Humanité, 1954, 1959).

For the military aspects of crusading see C. Oman, *A History of the Art of War in the Middle Ages* (rev. ed. 2 vols.; London, 1924); F. Lot, *L'Art Militaire et les armées au moyen âge en Europe et dans le proche Orient* 2 vols. (Paris, 1946); R. C. Smail, *Crusading Warfare (1097–1193),* with a good bibliography (Cambridge, 1956); R. Fedden and J. Thomson, *Crusader Castles* (London, 1950); C. Blair, *European Armour ca 1066 to ca 1700* (London, 1958).

For the crusader states and society, consult W. B. Stevenson, *The Crusaders in the East* (Cambridge, 1907); William Miller, *The Latins in the Levant; Essays on the Latin Orient* (Cambridge, 1921); J. L. La Monte, *Feudal Monarchy in the Latin Kingdom of Jerusalem* (Cambridge, Mass., 1932); C. Cahen, *La Syrie du nord à l'epoque des croisades et la principauté franque d'Antioch* (Paris, 1940); Sir George Hill, *A History of Cyprus* 3 vols. ([II–III "The Frankish Period, 1192–1571"], New York, 1948); J. Richard, *La Royaume Latin de Jerusalem* (Paris, 1953). The lectures of Bishop William Stubbs on "The Medieval Kingdoms of Cyprus and Armenia," in *Seventeen Lectures on the Study of Medieval and Modern History* (Oxford, 1886) are still useful.

H. Lamb, *Genghiz Khan* (New York, 1927), is a popular account touching on the Mongol conquests which has a selected, critical bibliography. See also M. Prawdin, *The Mongol Empire, its Rise and Legacy* (trans. from the German ed. of 1938: London, 1940); Christopher Dawson, *The Mongol Mission* (trans. of sources with intro.; London, 1955); J. J. Saunders, "Islam and the Mongols: the Battle of Goliath's Springs," in *History Today*, XI (1961) pp. 843–851, with short bibliography.

For the Muslims in the Levant consult P. K. Hitti, *History of the Arabs* (London, 1937). This same author has translated and edited the autobiography of Usama, published in Records of Civilization as *An Arab-Syrian Gentleman of the Crusades* (New York, 1929). This is most important for the Muslim point of view with regard to the crusaders in the Levant. There is a biography of Saladin by G. Slaughter (New York, 1955), which may be said to supersede the earlier one by Lane-Poole. In H. A. L. Gibb, *Studies in the Civilization of Islam* (Boston, 1962), are reprints of "The Armies of Saladin" and "The Achievements of Saladin," which were published originally in 1951–1952. In *Speculum*, XXXVII (1962) pp. 167–181 is an article "The Byzantines and Saladin, 1185–1192: Opponents of the Third Crusade" by C. M. Brand. See also, for the Assassins, an article by C. E. Nowell, "The Old Man of the Mountain," in *Speculum*, XXII (1947) pp. 497–519.

For the Spanish reconquest, the standard histories of Spain ordinarily will suffice, but special note may be taken of Ramon Menéndez Pidal's *La España del Cid*, 2 vols. (4th ed.; Madrid, 1947), which has been translated (from first ed.) in abridged form as *The Cid and His Spain* (London, 1934). See also Stephen Clissold, "El Cid: Moslems and Christians in Medieval Spain," in *History Today*, XII (1962), pp. 321–328, with short bibliography. For interpretation see Castro Américo, *The Structure of Spanish History* (Princeton, 1954). See also W. Starkie, *The Road to Santiago* (New York, 1957), and for Portuguese exploring, G. Renault, *The Caravels of Christ* (New York, 1959).

An approach to the crusades through fiction can be enlightening. Presumably Sir Walter Scott's novels *The Talisman* and *Count Robert of Paris* are more romantic than realistic, but the following recent works are recommended: A. L. Duggan's *Knight with Armour* (New York, 1950), which is about the First Crusade; the same author's *The Lady for Ransom* (New York, 1953), which treats of Byzantine mercenaries and the Manzikert campaign; and his *Lord Geoffrey's Fancy* (New York, 1962), which tells about the aftermath of the Fourth Crusade. Zoe Oldenbourg has two companion volumes dealing with feudal society whose members participate in the Third Crusade and the Albigensian Crusade, namely, *The World is Not Enough* (New York, 1948) and *The Cornerstone* (New York, 1955). She also has a novel about the Albigensian Crusade from the viewpoint of the heretics, *Destiny of Fire* (New York, 1961). In addition, she has written *Massacre at Montsegur: A History of the Albigensian Crusade* (New York, 1962).

In the *Cambridge Medieval History*, V (1929), chapter IX is entitled "The Effects of the Crusades upon Western Europe," to which is added the comment "the nature of the subject precludes a separate Bibliography." Discussion of the "results" of the crusades tends to embrace, one way or another, almost all late medieval culture. This makes bibliographical guidance very uncertain, but the following might be noted: C. H. Haskins, *Studies in the History of Medieval Science* (Cambridge, Mass., 1924) and his *The Renaissance of the Twelfth Century* (*Ibid.*, 1927). See also Sir Thomas Arnold and A. Guillaume, *The Legacy of Islam* (Oxford, 1931), N. A. Paris, ed., *The Arab Heritage* (Princeton, 1944), and H. A. L. Gibb, "The Influence of Islamic Culture on Medieval Europe," in *Bulletin of the John Rylands Library*, XXXVIII (1955–1956), pp. 82–98.

Bibliographical Supplement, 1969

Reconsideration of the Byzantine phases of the Christian-Muslim struggle will be found in the new vol. IV (Part I, 1966; Part II, 1967) of the *Cambridge Medieval History,* which is a newly written text replacing that of 1923 with a more up-to-date bibliography. Other titles more or less in this category are W. E. Kaegi, "The Contribution of Archery to the Turkish Conquest of Anatolia," *Speculum,* XXXIX (1964), pp. 96–108; C. Cahen, "An Introduction to the First Crusade," *Past and Present,* no. 6 (1954), with short bibliography. This is based on the same author's "En Quoi la Conquête Turque Appelait Elle la Croisade?" in the *Bulletin de la Faculté des Lettres de l'Univerité de Strasbourg,* (1950). Attention may also be called to W. M. Daly, "Christian Fraternity, the Crusades and the Security of Constantinople, 1097–1204; Precarious Survival of an Ideal," *Mediaeval Studies,* XXII (1960), pp. 43–91; C. M. Brand, *Byzantium Confronts the West: 1180–1204* (Cambridge, Mass., 1968). For Seljuks and Mongols consult the *Cambridge History of Iran,* vol. V, "The Saljuq and Mongol Periods" (London, 1969); and A. Bayer, "Edward I and the Mongols," *History Today,* XIV (1964), pp. 696–704.

The biography of Raymond of Toulouse by the Hills published in 1959 in Toulouse has been reissued recently by the Syracuse University Press.

For the Fourth Crusade we now have C. M. Brand, "A Byzantine Plan for the Fourth Crusade," *Speculum,* XLIII (1968), pp. 462-475; J. Folda, "The Fourth Crusade, 1201–1204; Some Reconsiderations," *Byzantino-Slavica,* XXVI, p. 177ff.; and C. Morris, "Geoffrey de Villehardouin and the Conquest of Constantinople," *History* (1968) pp. 24-34.

New translations of sources are J. H. and L. L. Hill, *Raymond d'Aguilers Historia Francorum qui ceperunt Iherusalem* (Philadelphia, 1968); Rosalind Hill, *Gesta Francorum et Aliorum Hierosolimitanorum* (London, 1962); and *Arab Historians of the Crusades* translated from Arabic into Italian by F. Gabrieli and from Italian into English by E. J. Costello (Berkeley, Calif., 1969).

Among the miscellaneous titles we note M. Mollat, "Problemes Mari-Times de l'Histoire des Croisades," *Cahiers de Civilisation Médiévale* (July–December, 1967); and R. J. Mitchell, *The Spring Voyage* (London, 1964). This last describes the Jerusalem pilgrimage of 1458. It is illustrated. There are excellent modern photographs in T. S. R. Boase, *Castles and Churches of the Crusading Kingdom* (London, 1967). For Muslim culture consult S. H. Nasr, *Science and Civilization in Islam* (Cambridge, Mass., 1968); also B. Lewis, *The Assassins: A Radical Sect in Islam* (New York, 1968).

For the Spanish reconquest we have R. I. Burns, *The Crusader Kingdom of Valencia; Reconstruction on a Thirteenth Century Frontier* 2 vols. (Cambridge, Mass., 1967). There is also the first critical modern history of one of the Spanish crusading orders: D. Lomax, *La Orda de Santiago, 1170–1275* (Madrid, 1965). For the earlier crusading orders in the Levant there are G. Legman, ed., *The Guilt of the Templars* (New York, 1966); and J. Riley-Smith *The Knights of St. John of Jerusalem and Cyprus,* vol. I to the transfer of the order to Rhodes (New York, 1967). A second volume is announced.

Index